"Carl Raschke has been one of the : _____ over the last quarter century. Here he provides a fresh appr... in and for theology, buttressed by critical engagements with Žižek and Badiou. Anyone interested in the vitality of contemporary theory should read this book!"
Clayton Crockett, University of Central Arkansas

"All good theology responds critically to the situation from which it emerges. Raschke's proposal for a new critical theology is no exception. For Raschke, our current postsecular condition is one in which religion functions as a public force in a pluralized world—a world that is riddled with sometimes violent contradictions. Responding to this condition requires not only taking religion seriously as a motivating factor in global conflicts, but also deploying it critically and politically toward universal, emancipatory ends. Raschke draws on recent work in Continental philosophy and critical theory—particularly the work of Alain Badiou and Slavoj Žižek—to provide an outline for such a theology. The result is both thought provoking and timely, and it should be required reading for those working in the fields of political theology, critical theory, and philosophy. Raschke's proposal, in short, sets an agenda that can't be ignored. Raschke's style also makes the book very accessible to a broader audience. He provides an admirably clear overview of twentieth-century critical theory and crisis theology as they relate to current issues regarding secularization, making this an ideal book to use in the classroom."
Hollis Phelps, University of Mount Olive, author of *Alain Badiou: Between Theology and Anti-Theology*

"In our globalizing world fraught with cultural, ideological and religious tension, the task facing Christian theology is both immense and urgent. Impressive in its scope and unflinching in its diagnosis of the current state of affairs, Carl Raschke's Critical Theology proposes a compelling theological agenda for an age of global crisis and asks with renewed vigor the old question, 'What has Athens (and Frankfurt, and Paris, and Ljubljana) to do with Jerusalem?' Raschke's deft critiques and provocative, constructive proposals blaze a promising path forward for radical theological analysis and engagement in our times."
Brent A. R. Hege, Butler University

"In *Critical Theology,* Carl A. Raschke provides a new and exquisitely detailed examination of critical 'global' thinking and its transdisciplinary connections to the legacy of postmodern theology and the future of an 'assembled' religious theory."
Victor E. Taylor, author of *Religion After Postmodernism*

"Often truth is the first casualty in a time of crisis. For Raschke, however, crisis is what most calls for truth. Unflinching in his commitment to argumentative clarity and undaunted by the enormity of the task of appropriating critical theory for political theology, Raschke offers a manifesto that is intellectually rigorous yet stylistically inviting. Anyone working in political theology will have to engage this book or risk ignoring the global crisis that calls for such theology in the first place."

J. Aaron Simmons, Furman University

Carl A. Raschke

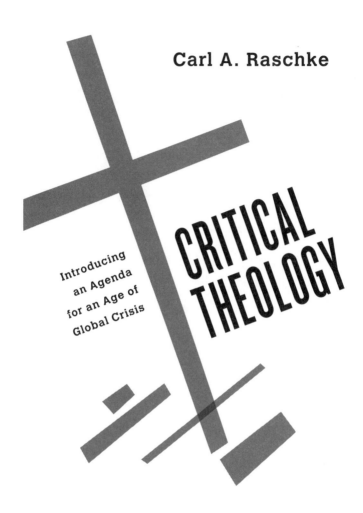

Introducing
an Agenda
for an Age of
Global Crisis

CRITICAL
THEOLOGY

IVP Academic

An imprint of InterVarsity Press
Downers Grove, Illinois

InterVarsity Press
P.O. Box 1400, Downers Grove, IL 60515-1426
ivpress.com
email@ivpress.com

InterVarsity Press® is the book-publishing division of InterVarsity Christian Fellowship/USA®, a movement of students and faculty active on campus at hundreds of universities, colleges and schools of nursing in the United States of America, and a member movement of the International Fellowship of Evangelical Students. For information about local and regional activities, visit intervarsity.org.

Cover design: Cindy Kiple
Interior design: Beth McGill
Images: paper texture: Ursula Alter/iStockphoto
  globe illustration: pijama61/iStockphoto

ISBN 978-0-8308-5129-4 (print)
ISBN 978-0-8308-9996-8 (digital)

Printed in the United States of America ∞

Library of Congress Cataloging-in-Publication Data
Names: Raschke, Carl A., author.
Title: Critical theology : introducing an agenda for an age of global crisis
 / Carl A. Raschke.
Description: Downers Grove : InterVarsity Press, 2016. | Includes
 bibliographical references and index.
Identifiers: LCCN 2016010702 (print) | LCCN 2016013662 (ebook) | ISBN
 9780830851294 (pbk. : alk. paper) | ISBN 9780830899968 (eBook)
Subjects: LCSH: Political theology. | Critical theory. | Christianity and the
 social sciences--History--21st century. | Religion and
 sociology--History--21st century. | Religion--Philosophy--History--21st
 century. | Theology--Methodology. | Postmodernism--Religious aspects.
Classification: LCC BL65.P7 R367 2016 (print) | LCC BL65.P7 (ebook) | DDC
 230--dc23
LC record available at http://lccn.loc.gov/2016010702

P	23	22	21	20	19	18	17	16	15	14	13	12	11	10	9	8	7	6	5	4	3	2	1
Y	36	35	34	33	32	31	30	29	28	27	26	25	24	23	22	21	20	19	18	17	16		

To my wife, Sunny,

and my family in the Netherlands—Erik and Jikke

as well as my grandchildren, Kes and Casjen

Contents

—

Preface

THIS FOLLOWING LITTLE BOOK constitutes an ambitious thought experiment that emerged from a casual blog post in the spring of 2014 in the international online publication *Political Theology Today*. The post concerning the need for a "new critical theology" caught the interest of editors at IVP Academic, and the development of this book project was the outcome. The idea of a "critical theology" of course was drawn from the familiar academic genre of "critical theory," first put forth by neo-Marxists in the 1920s in Germany before it migrated to America prior to the Second World War on account of Hitler's persecution of its main proponents. The article in *Political Theology Today* called attention to the rise of a new kind of critical theory represented by some of today's most famous philosophers from Continental Europe and social theorists who, like Karl Marx and Friedrich Engels themselves in the mid-nineteenth century, believed that the historical antecedents to the modern secular, revolutionary impulse could be found in Christianity and its struggle against the "principalities and power" that enslaved human beings at both a social and spiritual level.

The question that arose out of these peculiar ruminations was whether this preoccupation of the new interdisciplinary theorists with theological concerns could be considered a time for the emergence of a new "critical theology" from within the matrix of critical theory itself. A possible convergence of these "secular" interests, or what has previously been conceived in the theological mind—especially the evangelical Protestant one—as high-powered social and cultural critique, with the kind of

"deconstructive" faith-based analysis normally aimed at standard theological practices, institutions and modes of discourse, is a risky one. But
in just a decade or so we have all been thrust into the maelstrom of a
globalized world where the discussion of faith largely as a challenge for
the individual believer in the declining Western world has become less
and less compelling, or relevant. Every day in the headlines we encounter
the specter of a new worldwide sociopolitical volatility and instability,
demonstrating the fragility of the liberal world order that we have come
to take for granted in many of our lifetimes. Month after month the instability grows and has violent repercussions in the supposedly "safe
zones" that are the Western liberal democracies, as the accelerating pace
of terrorist attacks indicates.

The thesis of this project is complex, but also straightforward in many
respects. It is that the new era of global crisis demands a whole new
theological formulary that is unprecedented both in the content of the
challenges it faces and in the conceptual resources or "intellectual capital"
on which it must draw. These key resources are manifold, but they can
be tallied for the most part as follows: a deeper "biblical" understanding
of the meaning of divine incarnation, the ever-evolving legacy that has
come to be known as "critical theory," the insights of political thinking
and political theology, an updated theory of religions and "the religious,"
and finally the new, still somewhat amorphous body of suppositional
literature that deals with what is loosely termed *globalization*.

The response of the faithful to this new era of global of crisis as well as
global theorizing and global *theologizing* must be an unbending and au-
dacious one. Faith can no longer be "biblical" or confessional, as it has
been historically on the evangelical right. Nor can it simply be "dialectical"
or "socially and politically engaged," as has been the case on the
Protestant—and also in large measure Catholic—left. It cannot serve as
simply a brand marker for familiar ecclesiastical loyalties, or spiritualized
varnish for what are hardscrabble ideological commitments immune to
challenge or revision. A critical theology calls into question the very
framework of conventional theological analysis and theory production.

Furthermore, such a critical theology cannot merely remain "political" in the way that the endless procession of *au courant* civic theologies demand of us. It must make the "critical" turn in both a broad conceptual and practical fashion unlike what has been heretofore envisioned.

At the same time, a certain caveat should be registered here. The following does not by any stretch of the imagination pretend to be some detailed prospectus for a new critical theology of the type that so many scholars in today's cocooned and hothouse academic environment routinely look for. One cannot create a genre, or ignite a movement, by proclaiming either the urgency or the necessity of what we are self-consciously terming an "agenda" for the new age of global crisis. The rush of historical and international events that fracture and fatefully alter operative academic assumptions is becoming more intense by the day. Therefore, any proffered critical theology does not purport to offer comfortable, temporal "solutions," even with piecemeal applications, to the perceived permutations of the global crisis, but will have to develop organically from its own natural fibers and submerged root networks. But we can at least name these new tender shoots that may for the first time be pushing above the surface, and we can document and achieve some sort of inventory for the resources that might be required for such a large undertaking. The revival of "critical theory" in a broader sense than the term once connoted turns out to be one of the most significant events of the past decade, and it would be folly for the theologically minded (even if it is not the proper subject matter for self-established "theologians") to sidestep its importance for their deliberations.

The epoch in which we could spin out glib "theological" nostrums, whether we christen them "critical" or not, for whatever unsettles us came crashing down with the twin towers of the World Trade Center in September 2001. We can no longer just moralize, or intellectually dither, when confronted with the *reality*, including the frequent brutality, of what instantaneous digital communications bring constantly to our attention and often shock us with. As the philosopher Nietzsche wrote, we are "in the horizon of the infinite," whereupon "we have left the land and have gone aboard ship! We have broken down the bridge behind us . . . the land behind us! Well, little ship! Look out. Beside thee is the ocean . . . if homesickness for the land should attack thee, as if there had been more freedom there,—and there is no 'land' any longer."[1] That is a profound characterization of the era into which are sailing, and it is time our theological compasses were so adjusted.

Wings of the Eagle Retreat House
Southern Oklahoma
December 2015

Acknowledgments

I N THE DEVELOPMENT OF the preparation of this manuscript I would like to thank not only David Congdon and the editors of IVP Academic for inviting me to embark on this venture, but also for two special research assistants—Joshua Ramos and Timothy Snediker—whose contributions to both the mining of the literature and the framing of the issues and discourse, especially in the middle chapters, are not to be underrated. Finally, I would like to thank my son Erik for last-minute copyediting as well as my wife, Sunny, for her unflagging support and for allowing me time and space, mainly in the final hectic weeks, which included a death in the immediate family, to finish writing the book.

Small portions of this book originally appeared in the online publication *Political Theology Today* as well as *The Journal for Cultural and Religious Theory*.

1

Globalization and the Emergence of a New Critical Theory for the Age of Crisis

> *What can oppose the decline of the west*
> *is not a resurrected culture but the utopia that is*
> *silently contained in the image of its decline.*
>
> THEODOR ADORNO

THE NEW WORLD DISORDER

We are living in a time of profound global crisis in the Western world—one that is all at once economic, institutional, cultural, political and most of all religious. The crisis is visible everywhere around us. The abject failure of the Arab Spring as a political movement has fueled the sudden emergence of radical and ruthless Islamist ideologies like the Islamic State, bent on conquest, expansion and the genocidal extermination of its many enemies whom it lumps together as *kuffar,* or "unbelievers," which in turn have thrown the strategic assumptions of Western foreign policy into disarray. Within the Islamic world itself the "internationalization" of the long-standing Sunni-Shia antagonism and America's ambivalent, if not pusillanimous, role in shaping the conflict, has certainly added to the chaos. New geopolitical battles, or complex nationalist conflicts such as we find in Eastern Europe, are springing up everywhere and throwing into question the meaning and mettle of the Western democracies. Mean-while, the ever-deepening and toxifying chaos in countries like Syria and

Libya, prompted initially by well-meaning, ineffective half-measures on the part of Western governments to stave off genocide, have spawned even worse nightmares that now threaten the very structures of stable and prosperous nations, as the European refugee influx and the accelerating threat of terrorist attacks from the so-called Islamic State attests.

The prospects for a new global democratic order that seemed so promising in the 1990s now, as democracies wink out like decrepit stars from South America to Eurasia, seem at this point to have become something of a cruel joke. The lingering effects of the global financial crisis of 2008, which constantly threatens to break out again somewhere in the world in new and metastatic guises, cast an economic pall over what has become a deteriorating condition of the societies of the world everywhere we look. Between the moment this manuscript goes to press and its eventual publication we should not be at all surprised if some new and uncalculated dimension, if not *dimensions*, of the global crisis will have emerged. As the long-brewing "existential" threat to the European Union of Greece's debt default during the summer of 2015 showed, seemingly minor dislocations in the social and economic order can have massive potential repercussions. What a quarter century ago after the collapse of the Soviet Union seemed unmistakably to be the promise of what then President George H. W. Bush called the "new world order" is now the *new world disorder*. Although the Soviet Union is long gone, Russia has flexed its muscles aggressively once more. Civil society is fraying at the edges. In the United States, long considered the global signal fire for social progress and the hope of humanity, a combination of economic decline, toxic partisan division, a mood of religious apathy and moral rudderlessness, growing ethnic divisions, and isolationism when it comes to global leadership have accentuated the feeling that things are coming unglued.

It is not the first time in not-too-distant historical memory that the nations have teetered at the edge of unrivaled global crisis. During the late 1920s, as the world economy careened headlong toward economic disaster, a group of European thinkers and critics steeped in both German idealism and Marxist activism converged on Germany, at the

University of Frankfurt, to provide identity and notoriety for the recently established Institute for Social Research. Within time, the assemblage of now famous philosophers and cultural theorists associated with the institute, such as Jürgen Habermas,[1] Max Horkheimer,[2] Walter Benjamin,[3] Herbert Marcuse[4] and Erich Fromm,[5] came to be known as the *Frankfurter Schule* (Frankfurt school). The school, which in actuality was the epicenter of a worldwide intellectual movement that leveraged a broad, interdisciplinary method combining the humanities with the antipositivist social sciences and known as "critical theory," had a slow but powerful transformative impact on Western culture. Challenging every one of the dominant orthodoxies of its day, including fascism, Stalinist Marxism and corporate capitalism, critical theory was both directly and indirectly responsible for the various "cultural revolutions" of the 1960s that, in turn, profoundly reshaped the current Western academic and sociopolitical landscape.[6]

Critical theory embodied the age-old desire to combine thought with action, theory with practice. The Frankfurt school insisted that if any theory was to be deemed "critical," it had to insinuate a normative and potentially transfigurative constituency into its procedural apparatus. The Frankfurt school, in effect, traced its origins back to Kant's declaration that all critiques of knowledge must lead to the affirmation of human freedom, echoing of course Rousseau's celebrated manifesto for the age of revolution itself: "Man is born free; and everywhere he is in chains."[7] Thus Max Horkheimer proclaimed that the purpose of critical theory is "to liberate human beings from all circumstances that enslave them."[8]

The young Marx had demanded that philosophy must move from interpreting the world to changing it, but the Frankfurt school recognized that interpretation and change could not be easily disentangled from each other. Critical theory enlarged the domain of world-transforming praxis from political economy to a penetrating critique of culture itself, encompassing everything from an exposure of hidden structures of domination perpetuated by popular ideologies, to the analysis of the forms of communication and prevailing sign systems. The assumption was that effective political movements were impossible without a radical overhaul of the cognitive and moral frameworks within which every social agent operated.

The Frankfurt school became famous for its understanding of how communications media enslaves as well as emancipates. But with the exception of the ad hoc radical activism of students in the sixties with their tacit connections to its major theorists, it tended to avoid any deep-penetrating analysis of the role of educational institutions. Perhaps the oversight can be attributed simply to the relatively marginal role higher education in particular played as late as the 1950s in the formation of broader ideological commitments. But in the 2010s, when the Western economies were totally dependent on well-educated "cognitive workers," especially in the United States, with their astronomical amounts of student-loan debt threatening the sustainability of the entire system, a new burst of critical theory zeroed in on the increasingly dysfunctional interplay between the production of knowledge and the global hege-monies of the new corporate elites, while the importance of higher learning in such an equation at last seemed to be on everyone's radar. Various seminars and publications on what is coming to be known as the "new critical theory"[9] have sprung up, not to mention new forms of inter-disciplinary curricula at colleges and universities.[10]

These emergent instances of both high-level theory and committed praxis resemble to a certain degree what the influential contemporary French philosopher Alain Badiou has termed the "event." The "event," for Badiou, signifies a powerful disruption in the business-as-usual procedures within the corporate production of knowledge by the state-controlled edu-cational apparatus. The event pushes open a horizon for something wholly unanticipated and fraught with creative possibility that for the first time generates genuine "subjects," as Badiou says in his *Logics of Worlds*, who are fired with a sense of "destination," a vision of *truth*.[11] *L'événtement* is a sin-gularity disclosing the threshold of powerful and irresistible historical forces, like the Arab Spring itself (on which Badiou has written)[12] that are ready to break forth and transmogrify—perhaps almost overnight—a vast terrain. But before we venture into more detail about the new critical theory and its possibilities for engendering a new "critical theology" that might speak to the turmoil of our times, we might reflect on the historical circumstances the spawned the first iteration of such a critical theory as well as what might well count as the historical antecedents to the theological task, what was once known as "crisis theology."

WORLD WAR I AND ITS CONSEQUENCES

A little over a century ago in the summer of 1914, the murder of an Austrian archduke and his pregnant wife, by a teenage Serbian assassin, in the streets of Sarajevo in what was then the dual provinces of Bosnia and Herzegovina, set off an unexpected chain of events that led to the greatest social, military and political catastrophe the Western world had ever previously experienced. What we remember today as World War I was actually referred to at the time by many in Europe and America as "Armageddon," the long-prophesied climactic battle between God and the forces of darkness. It was the first truly global war, and in its deadly aftermath, there arose, for the first time in history, an awareness that a historical threshold had been crossed, that we had entered an epoch in which the efforts to identify and include vastly different peoples within a dawning planetary ethos amounted to something entirely new, something we now term *globalization*.

Historians are now slowly coming to realize that the magnitude and brutality of the four-year conflict, in which 17 million people perished, resulted not only from a sustained military gridlock manifested in the horrors of trench warfare but also from the crusading passions of both soldiers on the field and the civilian populations that waved flags in support while enthusiastically sending their youth to die en masse on distant battlefields. A violent clash of parochial and particularized passions generated an unprecedented debacle that left many questioning the old, familiar ways of knowledge and gave impetus to a profound sense of overarching crisis that Europe, and the rest of the world, had not experienced before. The lubricant for these lethal passions was by and large religious convictions that could not be disentangled from nationalist impulses.

The vast, mobilized militaries of Germany, England, France, Austria, Italy, America and Turkey all marched off into battle with an unassailable conviction that God was on their side and wanted them to emerge victorious in a war that, in the end, nobody really won. As Philip Jenkins writes, "Enthusiasm for the war was much greater than we might imagine," because the vast majority of combatants in each of the myriad armies that fought each other were all convinced that they "engaged in a war for righteousness' sake." Jenkins adds, "Contrary to secular legend, religious and supernatural themes pervaded the rhetoric surrounding the war. . . . If the war represented the historic triumph of modernity, the rise of countries 'ruled by scientific principles,' then that modernity included copious lashings of the religious, mystical, millenarian, and even magical."[13]

Once the war was finally concluded with an armistice in November 1918, however, the earlier "holy war" mentality gave way, both in Europe and America, to a profound disillusionment and cynicism. A year earlier the legions of peasant soldiers in the Russian army, who had sworn allegiance to "faith, Tsar and Fatherland," had been decimated on the Eastern front, only to return home to a revolution in the streets of Moscow. There they encountered a surprise seizure of power by a disciplined cadre of atheist, materialist "Bolsheviks," who declared the end of all nation-states and called for a worldwide uprising of the working classes as Karl Marx and Friedrich Engels had envisioned in *The Communist Manifesto* of 1848.

Vanquished, Germany itself almost went "red" following the armistice in the Spartacus Uprising of the winter of 1919, which was quickly crushed by government troops. The trauma of military defeat, combined with an overwhelming sense of humiliation on the part of much of the German population, by the terms of the war's settlement in the Versailles Treaty, led to the congenital dysfunctions of the Weimar Republic, its eventual breakdown and the ascendancy of Hitler and the Nazis in the early 1930s. Even in the victorious United States, which had not suffered nearly as many casualties as the European powers, the national mood was sullen, incredulous and rebellious. The now romanticized "Flapper Era," or the "Roaring Twenties," took to flaunting attitudes, values and behavior that hitherto had been considered Bohemian and antisocial due to the feelings of outrage and devastation that affected the psyche of so many Americans, especially the youth of that generation.

All things considered, the decades following World War I were characterized by a permanent sense of spiritual, moral and civilizational *crisis.* The apparent success of the Bolshevik Revolution of 1917 both terrified the middle classes, triggering waves of reactionary political movements such as the revived Ku Klux Klan in America and Mussolini's fascist blackshirts in Italy, and inspired the working classes, together with their ideological spokesmen and hangers-on, to a whole new level of militancy and insurrectionary fervor. When the Great Depression struck the developed world with unparalleled fury, the stresses of the immediate postwar period boiled over, resulting in seismic political upheavals from East Asia to the US Eastern Seaboard and eventuating in the Second World War. This thirty-year period of crisis and what came to be known as "total war" permanently and dramatically altered the cultural landscape of the West. But it also produced a heroism of radical new thinking that has left its lasting mark on thought and letters as well.

Neo-Kantianism and Its Discontents

Though Germany and Central Europe were in thorough political and social disarray during the decade after the Great War, it was also the occasion for some of the most creative intellectual ferment since the Napoleonic era, particularly in philosophy and theology. In the sleepy university town of Marburg, Germany, two giants of twentieth-century thought, the philosopher Martin Heidegger and his theological colleague Rudolf Bultmann, took on the hundred-year legacy of "neo-Kantianism." Neo-Kantianism was the dominant strand of German liberal thought throughout the nineteenth century, codifying and popularizing the complex philosophy of Immanuel Kant, the so-called sage of Königsberg, who wrote at the end of the Enlightenment of the eighteenth century.

German neo-Kantianism can be summarized broadly as an effort to rid philosophy of its "psychologist" or "subjectivist" tendencies, and to reconstitute it as a kind of *science of sciences*. Such an Olympian "science" (German = *Wissenschaft*) was far less concerned with empirical knowledge and more interested in what Kant himself had called the "pure understanding," best exemplified in logic, mathematics and the more formal disciplines of inquiry. But neo-Kantianism, particularly among those who followed Wilhelm Dilthey, and as embodied, for example, during the late nineteenth century in the "science of religions" movement, also had a strong interest in culture, moral values and the varieties of what the philosopher Ernst Cassirer referred to as "symbolic forms."[14]

Before Heidegger and Bultmann arrived on the scene, Marburg had been the fortified redoubt of neo-Kantian thought. Heidegger blasted neo-Kantianism for its facile scientism, which he claimed—famously—totally confused human theoretical constructs with the intimacy of human experience of what really is, or "beings" with "Being" itself. Similarly, Bultmann—often citing his colleague Heidegger—attacked the theological establishment for its glib identification of God as the presumed object of theology with the symbolic imagination and the various intellectual constructs that the "science of religions" had cobbled together to explain something called "religious experience." In the wake of the general postwar disorientation and malaise, both Heidegger and Bultmann chose a radically different starting point for their line of argument, which may be regarded as the broader touchstone for a contemporary "critical" approach to theological thinking. They set their compass by what they termed *Existenz*, or subjective existence, as Kierkegaard initially formulated it, the "facticity" of our simply "being there" in the world.

The new standpoint was not in any way the kind of "subjectivism" that earlier neo-Kantian *objectivists* had both caricatured and lambasted. It was the standpoint that gradually served as the rallying platform for the later "existentialist" movement as a whole—an intensive emphasis on the bare contingency of "being in the world," as Heidegger denominated it, on radical human freedom and on the necessity of personal decision. For Heidegger, the call to decision was a summons to "resolution" in the face of our eventual annihilation and amounted to a confrontation with the philosophy of the "meaning of being," which could only be apprehended in light of the possibility of total nonbeing, what he termed "being towards death."

For Bultmann, it was a call to respond to the overwhelming and incalculable reality of what the "word of God" presented to us in our contingent state, through the radical and *existential* decision of faith, a faith not buttressed at all by any guiding set of Christian doctrines or convictions, but by the reality of the gospel itself in its immediate demands on our whole being. In our subjective decision making, we are inevitably confronted with a *crisis*—not merely the crisis of belief, but the crisis of the possibility of our own nonbeing.[15] The trauma of widespread experience of trench warfare loomed large, one might speculate, in devising the controlling metaphors of the Heidegger-Bultmann venture.

That is not to imply Heidegger and Bultmann were not in any way at odds with each other. They were indeed, and what separated them was the tenacity with which each one clung to the primacy of his own field of inquiry—philosophy and theology. Both Bultmann and Heidegger departed from neo-Kantianism (although they both had been shaped and informed by it prior to the 1920s) because of what might be described as its comfortable and cozy identification of ultimate truth with scientific objectivity. But Bultmann and Heidegger diverged significantly from each other in regard to where they steered that critique. For Heidegger, the current crisis made it plain that the foundational question of all philosophy—Aristotle's quest in his *Metaphysics* for the meaning of "Being *qua* Being" —had been "forgotten," and it was now the urgent task of thinkers to "overcome" this profound and pervasive "amnesia" within the tradition. Theology, mired in its Christian dogmatic heritage, was incapable of acceding to the challenge. It was instead a question purely of "ontology," the thought of Being, a question only philosophy might address.

For Bultmann, on the other hand, only "theology" could take into serious account what had induced the crisis in the first place. Only theology could wrest meaning from the experience of the great trauma that the Western world had unexpectedly suffered. In his Pentecost sermon of 1917, Bultmann sketched the context for making this new kind of theological turn. He recalled his childhood celebration of Pentecost, the "birthday" of the Christian church itself in heritage and liturgy, as a "festival of joy." But he also invoked his recollections of Pentecost a year earlier when "I stood in a military hospital in the midst of the wounded and could hardly bring myself to say that Pentecost should be a festival of joy. Pain and misery stared at me out of large, questioning eyes, and the spirits of strife and alarm, of blood and terror, hovered oppressively throughout the room."[16] The lesson from that episode, Bultmann maintained, is that "if we want to see God, then the first thing we should say to ourselves is that we may not see him as we have conceived him. We must remind ourselves that he may appear *wholly other* than the picture we have made of him."[17]

The notion of God as "wholly other" had already been made famous as a category in the phenomenology of religion by the elder neo-Kantian Marburg scholar Rudolf Otto, even though it can be considered a general "eschatological" word that can be easily found in other Christian writers. Bultmann, however, took it not as a descriptive rubric but as an out-of-the-blue existential reality that throws into disarray any coherent cognitive system that we may have at our disposal to make our experiences intelligible to ourselves and to others. Our brute and bare finitude, our *Existenz*, is both contested and laid bare by such an encounter with the wholly other. Bultmann's later theology of the New Testament was built around the premise that biblical exegetes are always trying to commandeer the text with their own preconceptions about what it says, but that a genuine "existential" hermeneutic of Scripture allows the Word of God to confront us and drive deeply into our very flesh and bones, forcing us to respond in some dramatic fashion. His analysis was similar to John Calvin's "double knowledge of God," which he had laid out during the sixteenth century in his *Institutes of the Christian Religion*. According to Calvin, the more we understand the supreme and infinite majesty of God through reading Scripture, the more we are convicted of our own limitations, pridefulness and sinfulness. And the more we perceive our own "depravity," as Calvin put it, the more we acknowledge the glory of God.

Bultmann's "existential theology," his answer to Heidegger's *Existenz* philosophy,[18] can be construed as a partial precursor of what today we are beginning to understand as "critical theology." Bultmann's own "critical" approach lay in his uncompromising refusal to grant culturally conditioned conceptual constructs, which always find their way into the interpretive schemes we employ both to understand the Bible and to communicate the nature of Christian faith, to take precedence over the impinging presence and inestimable nature of the divine, what he himself in the Pentecost message termed the "force" of God. Bultmann's other well-known, but badly misconstrued, project of "demythologizing" the gospel had this controlling motive in mind. God's self-revelation to humankind in the Bible comes to be encrusted and weighed down, according to Bultmann, with a "world-picture" (my translation of the German word *Weltbild*, which he frequently uses) that needs to be discarded two millennia after the fact. The older world-picture needs to be stripped of its mythical and outmoded characteristics so that the genuine "message" or *kerygma* (Greek for "proclamation") of Scripture—the divine bidding to act obediently in faith—can be experienced on its own terms, in our own day.

But so much of Bultmann's approach, then as well as now, has been muddied by the ongoing controversy over the issue of world-picture, which he made a central theme in his project of "demythologizing." Moreover, Bultmann's thought remained within the mold of Lutheran pietism, focusing like the philosopher Søren Kierkegaard before him, and other religious "existentialists" who came afterward, on the stance of the lone believer before the inscrutable divine presence. What if the "crisis" out of which we are now charting a *critical theology* for our own day is one not so much of personal but of *social and cultural* existence? What if the "Word of God" stood over against not the varieties of personal idolatry and half-hearted belief but against the arrogance and pretensions of collective humanity itself?

Again, the devastating and world-destroying impact of the Great War, especially in Germany, had an even more powerful impression on a young Swiss theologian teaching in Germany. His name was Karl Barth. As a citizen of a country that remained neutral in both world wars, Barth was absolutely appalled at the way in which his teachers and colleagues rallied enthusiastically and without reservation around the war cause of the German Reich immediately following the mobilization in the summer of 1914. By the following year Barth had recognized the hidden dangers of the liberal theological framework within which so much theological thinking up until that time was conducted.

Germany's unvarnished and unapologetic cultural nationalism was disclosed when so many prominent German intellectuals publicly endorsed the war aims as a marvelous crusade to preserve the unique "spiritual" heritage of their country against the barbarous Anglo-Saxon onslaught. Even before the war reached its tragic denouement, therefore, ending in German defeat, Barth had launched a one-man revolt against what was, in effect, the entirety of nineteenth-century Continental religious thought. His revolt, which initially drew on what he considered the profound "dialectical" power of the apostle Paul's arguments in the book of Romans, came to be known as "crisis theology." The historical crisis itself was but a clear and obvious demonstration, to all concerned, that God had executed judgment (Greek = *krisis*) on the world and that the biblically prophesied kingdom of God was breaking in. As Barth would write, "The affirmation of *God, man,* and the world given in the New Testament is based exclusively upon the possibility of a new order absolutely beyond human thought; and therefore, as prerequisite to that order, there *must come a crisis that denies* all human thought."[19]

As Gary Dorrien observes, such a "sentiment was appealing to many pastors and academics in the aftermath of the war. They were finished with Christian arguments for the support or renewal of German society, at least for the time being. Like Barth, some were repulsed by the spectacle of war experience theology [and] . . . were chastened enough by this spectacle to question the entire trend of the past generation toward an increasingly politicized culture-religion."[20] Crisis theology was ruthlessly *critical* of any theological attempt to correlate Christian claims and cultural experience. Even Bultmann's more radical type of correlationism Barth came to dismiss as covertly captive to the finite dimensions of human knowledge mapped by philosophical inquiry. "Existence," even though it purported to call into question all human constructs, was still exactly that—a construct! The only genuine, noncorrelative reality by which theologians might set their course was the "Word of God," an expression Barth employed tirelessly not so much in the sense of its Reformed connotation as scriptural revelation, but as God's *absolute self-disclosure* of his own sovereign prerogative. For Barth, even those staple elements of Catholic doctrine that Protestants considered as derivative from Scripture, such as the Trinity, the Chalcedonian unity of God and man in the person of Christ, and so on, could be regarded as "revelation" in the direct sense of the term.

Barth's take-no-prisoners approach to theological issues was upsetting to his contemporaries, to say the least. Bultmann and Barth eventually parted ways, even though both of them, as Christophe Chalamet convincingly shows, were faithful in their own way to the method of "dialectical theology" (the insistence that revelation includes both a "yes" of affirmation regarding God's saving Word and a "no" when it comes to the pretensions of human thought, including theology).[21] It appears Bultmann by 1930 had simply become tired of Barth's bombast, even though the constraints of thinking and writing during the thirties and forties may have had a lot do with it. However, from a historical standpoint the theological nuances of the controversies and contentions of the 1920s and 1930s were eclipsed on the world's historical stage, especially by what had been going on since World War I in *social thought* as a whole. Interestingly, up until Germany's humiliation in 1919 many of its well-known theological luminaries had been moderate socialists, with a typical commitment to what today we would call "liberal politics," in its preoccupation with the welfare of the working class and a penchant for limited state intervention when it amounted to promoting the common good. The theological disengagement from progressive politics after 1919 was the outgrowth of the utter disillusionment across Europe with "social democracy," parliamentarianism and the various forms of political meliorism. The road to hell was now seen as paved with good intentions, and even the most exemplary strategies of progressivism were perceived as profoundly tainted by human corruption and self-seeking.

Meanwhile, the unexpected outcome and aftermath of the Russian Revolution was just as telling in the shaping of attitudes among the postwar generation. The events of October 1917—what American journalist and Communist sympathizer John Reed termed the "ten days that shook the world"—were perceived at first with ambivalence by onlookers in the West. Social radicals, like Reed, who later snuck into Russia to become the Revolution's key external spokesman, hailed the Bolshevik coup as the apocalyptic realization of a decades-long longing for an insurrectionary blow against global capitalism. Garden-variety Democrats as a whole were at best dubious and at worst aghast. Political conservatives, of course, were incensed. By the end of the 1920s, however, the widespread suffering of the people in Russia, due to the ongoing upheavals and the reported brutalities of the emerging Stalinist regime, had a sobering impact on all but the most diehard Communist ideologues, who nevertheless remained quite numerous. The abiding hope among Western intellectuals that the social injustices of the capitalist system might be turned around through collective activism and the impact of real historical events did not die easily. As the idealism of the postwar "red" sympathizers slowly waned, the elements of a new secular method of both cultural critique and social action began to absorb the energies of those yearning for a transformation of things.

THE COMING OF THE FRANKFURT SCHOOL

The catastrophic economic collapse of the 1930s was the main catalyst for this shift. No matter one's own religion or politics, it became impossible to avoid any longer what was called the "social question." The "theology of crisis," as it had been laid out after the war, as well as the Bultmannian-

Heideggerian hermeneutics of *Existenz,* now seemed painfully abstract and arcane in many respects. What had increasingly garnered attention throughout the 1920s was an alternative to both theology and orthodox Marxism that came to be known as "critical theory." The earlier critical theorists were, by and large, German-Jewish intellectuals who had lost their standing among Marxist revolutionaries after the failure of the Spartacus Rebellion in 1918 and after fading in the face of the new glamour accorded to the nascent Soviet experiment. Marxist theory had predicted the inevitability of a successful revolution in Germany rather than in backward feudal lands such as Russia. But the precise opposite had indeed transpired. Thus the academically entrenched German socialist intelligentsia, having been forced to accept the "bourgeois compromise" of the Weimar Republic as well as have it cast aside as inconsequential by actual, on-the-ground revolutionaries in other parts of the world, found themselves having to rethink Marxism almost in its entirety. This radical revisioning of Marxist dialectics in accord with the postwar situation in Europe, especially with the grim menace of fascism ever on the rise, was the task of what today we would call a "think tank," known as the Institute for Social Research, founded in 1923 at the University of Frankfurt.

Throughout the 1920s and until the mid-1930s, when the institute was disbanded by the Nazis and its principals driven into exile in the United States, the Frankfurt school (a name associated with the body of writings by thinkers connected to the institute) sought to recover the "humanist" dimension of revolutionary socialism by delving into the newly discovered *Economic and Philosophic Manuscripts* of the young Marx. The Frankfurt school thus at the same time succeeded in relocating Marxist social analysis, in the rich philosophical tradition of German idealism, starting with Kant and culminating in Hegel. Like the crisis theologians, who were their immediate contemporaries, the early critical theorists developed a form of dialectical thinking that constantly called into question the assumptions and ideological pretensions of their academic contemporaries.

Crisis theology and *critical theory* from their inception had one very important thing in common: a resistance to glib theoretical justifications of the existing order and grand metaphysical explanations of the why and wherefore of things, even those of the "historical materialist" variety championed by orthodox Marxists. Crisis theology wanted to liberate the cultural mind from pseudostrategies of collective redemption so that God could be "free," as Luther put it, "to be God" in dealing with the human condition. Critical theory aimed to clear away once and for all the rubbish of all-encompassing materialist, mechanistic, scientistic and idealistic accounts—what the French philosopher Jean-François Lyotard once named "grand narratives"—so that the goal of both secular utopians and religious prophets through the ages could at least be proximately achieved—that is, a new birth of freedom and the end of servitude and alienation, as Horkheimer envisioned.[22]

Once it had been uprooted from Europe and set up residence at Columbia University in New York in the second half of the 1930s, critical theory, as now conceived, began to take clear shape. The dominant influence on the new project of critical theory during this period, in contrast with earlier efforts to reinterpret Marxism from a more humanistic perspective, was Herbert Marcuse. Marcuse joined the institute in 1932, a year before it was shut down by the Nazis. He would later become famous in America during the social turmoil of the 1960s and early 1970s as the reputed "father of the New Left," not only because of the popularity of his writings with the radical activists of that era, but also on account of his involvement in major public protests and his willingness to speak out in favor of certain kinds of "revolutionary" social action. He was even accused regularly of advocating violence, although the evidence to back that claim is muddied, to say the least. What Marcuse offered, however, was a fusion of European Hegelianism and academic Marxism, on the one hand, with the Frankfurt school's central preoccupation after the move to America, namely popular culture, on the other hand. When additional expertise in psychoanalysis was provided by Erich Fromm, another Jewish refugee from Hitler's Germany, at about the same time, the stage was set for the Frankfurt school to erect the scaffolding for what would become so much of interdisciplinary "theory" in the arts and humanities in America from the seventies onward. What exactly is, or was, critical theory in this context? Marcuse, who largely was responsible for coining the expression, characterized it as something quite different from "social theory," in which orthodox Marxism was anchored, as well as from philosophy in its historic sense. The *critical* function of critical theory, according to Marcuse, is played by the omni-operational force of "reason," a notion he derives straightaway from Hegel.

For Hegel, the dialectical movement of rationality in human thought, and in concrete historical life, is propelled by what Hegel termed the "power of the negative." In what were very well-researched and masterfully argued writings on the political relevance of Hegelian dialectic, especially his 1941 tome *Reason and Revolution*, Marcuse insisted that "negativity is manifest in the very process of reality, so that nothing that exists is true in its given form."[23] The upshot, of course, is that critical theory maintains the thrust of the "negative" from an immanent, theoretical position, in much the same way that Barth's divine *Nein* served as the engine of dialectical, or crisis, theology. However, even though Marcuse developed his idea of critical theory from a close reading of Hegel's *Logic*, the "revolutionary" impetus of historical reason emanates not from the momentum of self-negating concepts in the process of transmutation but from the character of social and economic reality itself.

For Marcuse, therefore, there could be no distinction between "dialectical materialism"[24] and a hypothesized *dialectical idealism*, insofar as they are, from the sociohistorical vantage point, one and the same. It is this lack of distinction, when it comes to dialectics, that separated critical theory from both the party-controlled Communist orthodoxy of Soviet times and the armchair *academic and cultural Marxism* that prevails nowadays. Critical theory has a key social and operational dimension to it, which the other forms supposedly lacked as well, in what we might dub an "ethical dimension," drawing on the universalism of Kant's *categorical imperative*,[25] which was central to the idea of "pure practical reason" at the heart of the latter's own "critical philosophy."[26] Indeed, critical theory *is* a kind of critical philosophy in a much broader sense, according to Marcuse, if not to the whole of philosophy itself. "The interest of philosophy," Marcuse later wrote, "found its new form in the interest of critical social theory. There is no philosophy alongside and outside this theory. For the philosophical construction of reason is replaced by the creation of a rational society."[27]

The vision was close to Plato's ideal of a republic, where philosophers ruled, with the exception that in Marcuse's utopia philosophers would be kings only because they had raised the self-consciousness of society to the point that revolutionary transformation would come from the masses' own immanent "critical" reasoning and desire for a new order of things. Marcuse's Hegelian take on the anatomy of revolution became the hidden catalyst for the uprisings of the sixties, which were almost always seeded within the systems of mass higher education and anticipated in rhapsodies of the coming of the new "knowledge society" that were not on anyone's radar prior to the Second World War.

CRITICAL THEORY COMES OF AGE

Marcuse's star faded with the end of the political turmoil of the Vietnam era, and the reputation of a younger associate of the Frankfurt school by the name of Habermas, who quickly rose in the firmament. Unlike earlier spokespersons for critical theory, Habermas was from a traditional German Protestant family whose patriarch was reportedly a Nazi sympathizer. Moreover, Habermas was born in 1929 and was merely a young boy throughout the Nazi era. He never was compelled to go into exile, and completed his graduate education in the de-Nazified, liberal democratic environment of West Germany during the 1950s, even though his mind was extensively shaped by the thought of Adorno and Horkheimer, his teachers at the now revived Institute for Social Research at the University of Frankfurt. The entirely different social and institutional context in which Habermas elaborated his own version of "critical theory" should not be underestimated. In comparison with his elders who had experienced the sudden descent of democracy into malignant and militarized fascism, Habermas came to believe in the future of a new post-Nazi and self-consciously cosmopolitan Europe. Thus, while riding all the postwar intellectual and philosophical currents of his time, Habermas's thought, over time, became a *force maieur* for legitimizing Western democracy. As Agnes Heller puts it, Habermas's "Marxism" was from the outset an "institutionalised one" with its standard academic gestures in the direction of "historical materialism."[28]

What was also missing in Habermas's take on critical theory, according to Heller, was any interest in the emancipatory potential of the proletariat, which he, like many so-called cultural Marxists who would later come to the forefront in the sixties through the influence of Marcuse, was convinced had now lost their revolutionary fire and turned socially conservative. The regime of capital cannot be overthrown through any kind of mobilized collective wrench thrown into its whirring wheelworks. Instead it has to do it through a "gradual" process of self-education and what in the 1960s came to be known simply as "consciousness-raising." Such consciousness-raising, offered as the premise of any manner of liberating praxis, depends not on any forced indoctrination of the masses, as had become the general rule in the totalitarian societies of orthodox Marxism that had sprung up from 1948 onward from China to Cuba (and of course in the Soviet Union). Instead it must rely on self-education, what South American educational theorist Paolo Freire would label the "pedagogy of the oppressed." It would be the consequence of a *critically transformed* method of social transactivity in which collective action cannot be distinguished from intersubjective communication. Habermas would name this new methodology a "theory of communicative action." Not only would the theory of communicative action gradually in Habermas's oeuvre replace the doctrine of historical materialism as the key to emancipatory praxis, but it would also reverse the conventional Marxist, together with fascist and to a less extent social democratic, suspicions of the capacity of political democracy. "The idea of a domination-free communication," Heller writes, "related to the emancipatory interest of everyone can be properly described as 'radical democracy.'"[29]

What exactly was "critical" in Habermas's account of critical theory? To answer that question, we have to go back to Horkheimer's distinction between "traditional" and "critical" theory. In a key essay composed in the late 1930s he observed that the "goal of all theory" ultimately is "a universal systematic science, not limited to any particular subject matter but embracing all possible objects."[30] Horkheimer subsequently makes the point that such systemization since the advent of the modern epoch has been consigned to the mathematical sciences, following Descartes's vision of a complete epistemology applicable to all observed phenomena in the form of a *mathesis universalis*, or a "universal mathematical formalization." He also salutes the prestige of this "traditional" theoretical position by citing the rush of the nineteenth-century social sciences to ape the Cartesian model when it comes to human behavior, a protocol that even Marx in part was conscientious about obeying.

In German philosophy, such a program of formalization, however, was dependent less on conjuring effective sets of algebraic markers or notional symbols than on establishing, from the standpoint of what Kant had called a "transcendental logic," the absolutely certain grounds of knowledge, from which the "objective" attributes of empirical phenomena could be deduced. So much of Kant's famous *Critique of Pure Reason* is dedicated to sketching the conditions of knowledge under which these attributes can be both investigated and warranted. In other words, Kant carried forward Descartes's attempt to identify the very principles by which "science" as a framework of "clear and distinct ideas" might possibly be authorized, although he did so in a much more deliberate, detailed, nuanced and scholastic style of writing and argumentation. What the later German philosopher Edmund Husserl, inventor of the method known as "phenomenology," would call the "transcendental" standpoint, as opposed to the "natural attitude" of everyday consciousness, became the starting point for the whole of traditional "theory" with its various connotations and ramifications, which the Frankfurt school had inherited.

At the same time Kant's well-known "transcendental reduction," which so much of German philosophy took for granted, had been upended by

Hegel's "dialectical" model, on which Marxism as a form of revolutionary theory and praxis intimately depended. Much of German idealism, which includes the writings of Husserl, has in effect—as the latter made us aware in his *Cartesian Meditations*—sought to solve the classical philosophical problem of the subject-object distinction in much the same fashion as Descartes himself attempted by laying out the conditions under which *subjective certitude* can be established. Hegel, on the other hand, realized that the subject-object distinction is not really a distinction at all, insofar as the conditions of subjective certitude are inherently tied up with the interplay between self-consciousness and what is present to consciousness itself as external, or ulterior. Hence self and not-self are part of an in-severable bond and constitute an irresolvable tension within consciousness. Our awareness of ourselves and our awareness of objects are merely dependent on which temporal moment we find ourselves in when we try to overcome this tension. Hegel called this "movement" of consciousness, from self-awareness to recognition of what is "other than" consciousness, and back to a final realization that self and other form an unbreakable dyad, the "dialectic," borrowing a well-worn term from the history of philosophy and giving it a radically new meaning.

For Hegel, the "dialectic" became a technical term whereby self-consciousness and consciousness of the "other" could be construed as higher-order perspective on what we have in mind when we are talking about "consciousness" in general, especially when it comes down to the fact that we all share as social and linguistic beings the same terrain of human experience. As the twentieth-century philosopher Ludwig Wittgenstein would affirm, there can be no such thing as a "private" consciousness apart from madness, and more importantly there can be no such thing as a private language corresponding to that putatively private self-awareness. The ongoing social and historical transformations in this intersubjective expanse of meaning and consciousness Hegel named "Spirit."

Marx belonged to a cohort of next-generation German philosophers who came to be known as the Young Hegelians. The Young Hegelians were not so much interested in expounding on the subtleties of Hegelian "idealism" as they were devoted (in Marx's immortal words) to turning their master "on his head." For Marx, the dialectical movement of consciousness therefore was interpreted as the intrinsic pattern for the ongoing transformations of the material sphere, especially when it came to what he termed "the relations of production," or the prevailing forms of social and economic existence. Marx considered the Hegelian notion of Spirit a "mystification," which both concealed and belied the dialectical "contradictions" within the social and economic order of things. These contradictions for the most part centered on the historical "struggle" between different social classes—mainly the "bourgeoisie" with their control of capital and the proletariat, or working class, which have nothing but their labor—who have been able to commandeer in an unequal manner the "means" and "forces" of production.

In anticipation of the analytical vantage point that would a century later be regarded as "critical theory," Marx insisted, especially in his earlier works, that the philosophical "clarity" of consciousness means nothing unless it has been *clarified* as "class consciousness," that is, unless it has become self-aware of the profound tensions within the material circumstances of life that are easily misidentified and self-deceptively misunderstood merely as ideations, or as mental phenomena. Once one realizes that the conceits of philosophers are little more than "projections" of these underlying material contradictions and that they constitute an "ideological" superstructure serving as an overlay for a hidden material substructure, philosophy will no longer be "reflection" on the nature of things, but a goad to social transformation and revolutionary praxis. As the inscription on Marx's grave goes (which he took from one of his earlier writings), "the philosophers have only *interpreted* the world, in various ways. The point, however, is to *change* it."

In promulgating his specific canons of critical theory, Horkheimer built on this notion that the "critical" in all critical theory hinges on the reinterpretation of the "transcendental" standpoint as a method of challenging the existing order, rather than finding reasons for justifying it. The leverage of the "ideal" in German idealism thus could be taken as a realization that the way things are needs to be judged (*krinein*) with respect to what one can envision from a timeless value-perspective. Critical theory, which in many ways was heavily dependent on Kant's moral and social philosophy, revolved around the latter's essential distinction between the *was ist* ("what is the case") and *was soll* ("what ought to be"). The idea of the "transcendental" became the consummate standard for demanding that the world itself be changed in a powerful and distinctive manner.

As a result, critical theory supersedes traditional theory insofar as it promotes an "active subject," according to Horkheimer, who is invested materially, culturally and intellectually in his or her situation and is no longer a passive spectator. Critical theory *activates* the Kantian "transcendental ego" as well and makes it into a formative dynamic within the world at large.

> At least Kant understood that behind the discrepancy between fact and theory, which the scholar experiences in his professional work, there lies a deeper unity, namely, the general subjectivity upon which individual knowledge depends. The activity of society thus appears to be a transcendental power, that is, the sum-total of spiritual factors.[31]

Or, as Martin Jay in his groundbreaking history of the Frankfurt school sums up the matter, critical theory "refused to fetishize knowledge as something apart from and superior to action. . . . It recognized that disinterested scientific research was impossible in a society in which men were not yet autonomous; the researcher . . . was always part of the social object he was attempting to study."[32]

EMERGENCE OF A NEW CRITICAL THEORY

Today, most scholars and ambitious lay readers treat the Frankfurt school and its critical theory primarily as an intellectual museum piece, or largely as a source of inspiration from the past. The last blast of the Frankfurt school was the mobilization of young radicals and social change makers, often driven by theological convictions, in both Europe and America from the mid-1960s to approximately the end of the 1970s. Yet the quest to make human beings "autonomous," as Jay puts it, has not ebbed at all in the intervening years. The search for a new, general theory that will combine a searching and penetrating critique of the present order of things, with an "emancipatory" strategy that weds theory skillfully with praxis, as the Frankfurt school strove to accomplish, continues unabated, and in recent years has found a sundry set of voices in contemporary philosophy who in turn have become celebrities for the emerging generation we know as millennials.

Some of these new academic celebrities, like Badiou himself, cut their conceptual wisdom teeth during the political turmoil of the Vietnam era. As a young student radical with strong Communist affiliations (as was normal at the time for most French intellectuals), Badiou participated in a number of different uprisings and mobilizations in France, especially the now famous events of early May 1968. Although short-lived and marginal in their overall consequences, these events have sometimes been called, perhaps with undeserving hyperbole, the "third French Revolution" or, with a little more modesty, the "Twentieth Century Paris Commune." Many at the time, including Badiou himself, referred to May 1968 as *l'événement* because of the fashion in which it seemed to crystallize out of nothing, then dissipate immediately, as if it had never really taken place. What made "the event" so astonishing was that, unlike student movements and so-called youthquakes in other parts of the world, the turbulence of May 1968 conjured a transient alliance between disaffected young people, organized labor and even professional associations. As a result, it came quite close to forcing from power the seemingly entrenched, postwar Gaullist government and fulfilling the much earlier, revolutionary ideal of the "general strike" that had first been envisioned by the French syndicalist Georges Sorel many decades earlier. It was these experiences that prompted Badiou to make the theory of the event the lodestar of his entire philosophical project. Later in his career Badiou would make the case that the event cannot be separated from what we would term its "religious" or "theological" dimensions, even though he adamantly refused to let go of his long-standing materialist, Marxist and atheist commitments.

It is for this reason also that Badiou—and certain other important contemporary thinkers, some of whom are no longer alive—can be deemed the vanguard of the *new critical theory*. The new critical theory bears strong affiliations with the old critical theory, inasmuch as it melds radical social analysis, often leveraging some version of Marxist thought, with a profound interest in the critique of culture and even with, as we might dare term it, a radical "religious" interest. It is this religious interest, which we find to some degree in all the new critical theorists, that not only distinguishes decisively the new from the old but points to a *theological* interest as well. It is because of this decidedly theological motivation in so much of the new critical theory that we can begin to conceive of the possibility of an actual "critical theology" that brings about a coalescence of both the uncompromising faith stance of the earlier "crisis theology" and the systematic social, cultural and psychological concerns of the Frankfurt school.

It is not my aim in this book to do anything approaching a comprehensive survey of both the old and new critical theorists. For our purposes we will concentrate mainly on two very important and currently living figures—Badiou and the Slovenian philosopher Slavoj Žižek. Other so-called postmodern philosophers who draw the attention of students of the new critical theory—for example, Gilles Deleuze, Michel Foucault and Jacques Rancière—can be easily located within this constellation, and thus they should be investigated diligently if one wants an understanding of the scope of this next generation of critical theorizing.

Furthermore, as we shall discover in later chapters, even the trajectory of thinking for certain philosophers such as Habermas should be regarded as part of the new critical theory. Nor do I intend to explore the impressive and complex elements, as well as ramifications of the thought, of the two figures I have already singled out. What we must look at instead is the way in which critical theory, which because of dogmatic Marxism rejected out of hand the religious dimension, *now requires it*. And from this starting point we can begin to sketch the lineaments, though not really the denser specifics, of that "theology of the future" we will without equivocation name as *critical*.

The Need for a New Critical Theology

*Man is not imprisoned by habit. . . . Great
changes in him can be wrought by crisis—once
that crisis can be recognized and understood.*

NORMAN COUSINS

CRITICAL RESPONSE IN AN AGE OF CRISIS

Whether it is actually the best of times or the worst of times or somewhere in between, a seemingly irresistible parlor game for pundits, does
not count as much as the general *perception* that a deep and far-reaching
crisis is unfolding. Now that the euphoria of the 1990s over the end of
the Cold War and the rosy prospects for democracy and the expansion
of market economies have shriveled into yellow, cracked scraps of
parchment, the new pessimism provides immense opportunity for the
making of Norman Cousin's "great changes." Crisis thinking has always
been the flair of those who wind up making a significant difference in
the world. Recognizing that there is a crisis itself is the task of competent
thinkers. Understanding the origins, complexity and interworkings of
the crisis requires even further talent and skill. Those thinkers, or religious geniuses, who arise from time to time and whom we name
"prophets" demonstrate the capacity for both such discernment and
analysis. Even more broadly speaking, we call this kind of probing in-
sightfulness "critical thinking" or "critical intelligence."

The terms *crisis* and *critical*, of course, derive from the Greek *krinō*, meaning "judgment." A critical mindset is one with an inherent ability to discern and comprehend things that the ordinary person would overlook, ignore or refuse to accept as contrary to "common sense." Critical thought, inevitably, is met with strong resistance, particularly among those who share much of the same world picture and system of assumptions. That regrettable truth lies behind Jesus' famous saying that a "a prophet is not without honor except in his own town, among his relatives and in his own home" (Mk 6:4 NIV). It is in the very nature of a crisis that most people do not see things or "connect the dots" in the same manner as the prophet, or critical thinker. Sudden or anomalous events are construed in a more conventional manner, thus impairing the effectiveness of the leader, or decision maker, who might be able to act with deliberation and determination, in doing the right thing, and having any kind of calculable impact on the situation. A renowned historical illustration is the reaction of the French monarch Louis XVI to the news that a mob had ransacked the state prison in Paris known as the Bastille in 1789. "It is a revolt?" Louis inquired rather insouciantly, knowing that uprisings among the population were not at all uncommon and usually ended in brutal suppression by royal agents. "Nay, sire," came the reply. "It is a revolution!"[1] Because Louis XVI neither discerned that a revolution was brewing, nor had any idea of how to stop it once it was in full sway, he literally lost his head.

Celebrated twentieth-century political theorist Hannah Arendt, student and lover of the even more famous philosopher Martin Heidegger, exhibited such "critical" insight. An award-winning movie about her life, produced in 2012 by German filmmaker Margarethe von Trotta, focuses on how the Jewish philosopher, who was already quite famous for her work on the Nazi phenomenon *The Origins of Totalitarianism*, laid bare for the first time, in a series of onsite reports on the trial in Israel of Adolf Eichmann, the personality and motivations of one of the masterminds of the Holocaust, or what the Nazi hierarchy dubbed the "Final Solution." After carefully observing Eichmann's testimony, she drew the highly unpopular conclusion that he was not some larger-than-life evil genius, but a mindless bureaucrat who appeared to be simply doing his job and executing orders from above, like any middle manager, in authorizing mass exterminations of Jews and others the Nazis marked for genocide. In her literary dissection of his modus operandi in her book *Eichmann in Jerusalem*, Arendt minted the phrase, which has become almost a cliché over the years, the *banality of evil*, which referred to the glib ease with which Eichmann could rationalize away, and deny responsibility for, his monstrous crimes against humanity.

When the book appeared in 1963, many of Arendt's former admirers were incensed over what they considered her all-too-detached attitude regarding Eichmann's motives, and they publicly denounced her. Even many of her faculty colleagues at the New School for Social Research in New York wanted her relieved of her teaching duties. But Arendt stuck by her convictions and, as dramatized in the movie, gave a powerful and moving defense—what the Greeks and early Christians termed an *apologia*—for why she had made the case about Eichmann in the way she did. The seed of "radical evil" in Eichmann and his actions, according to Arendt, was due neither to some demonic pathology nor to a willful perversity, but to Eichmann's cluelessness about, and open refusal of, the demand to *think*. Arendt's preoccupation with the power and importance of thinking came directly from Heidegger, who in his last series of university lectures in 1951 to students at the University of Freiburg delivered the memorable line, "Most thought-provoking in our thought-provoking time is that we are still not thinking." A few lines later Heidegger clarifies this mantra-like statement throughout the lectures with the following observation: "This [assertion] now means: We have still not come face-to-face, have not yet come under the sway of what intrinsically desires to be thought about in an essential sense."[2]

Arendt, the Jew, of course took the challenge of thinking in a wholly different direction than Heidegger, the German who flirted briefly with Nazism. For Heidegger, the unthought of thought is the meaning of Being itself, the most fundamental question of philosophy. For Arendt, the challenge comes down to devising the courage for a most radical kind of

thinking and the risky decisions accompanying it, especially when confronted with fateful political choices, or the moral dilemmas of life and
death. Thinking, therefore, is never abstract, but occurs in the exigency
of the lived moment. As Arendt herself stressed, thought always situates
itself within the perplexities of our experience. And these perplexities can
sometimes be overwhelming, where if we make the wrong call (as in the
parable of the "The Lady, or the Tiger?," in which a man who is asked to
select a door to open behind which may be lurking either a beautiful
woman to coddle him or a ferocious beast to devour him), the consequences may be devastating. Real thinking, therefore, as Bethania Assy
notes in her analysis of Arendt's philosophy, inheres in what Immanuel
Kant designated the "faculty of judgment," not a logical judgment, where
we reason from the general to the particular and back to the general, but
from the crisis to a choice of principles by which we make the proper
response and back to a deeper understanding of the crisis itself.

As Arendt herself insisted with a panache that was captured in the
concluding dramatic scene of the movie, in which she lays out her defense for what she wrote about Eichmann,

> If thinking . . . actualizes the difference within our identity as given in con-
> sciousness and thereby results in conscience as its by-product, then *judging*,
> the by-product of the liberating effect of thinking, realizes thinking . . . in the
> world of appearances, where I am never alone and always too busy to be able
> to think. The manifestation of the wind of thought is not knowledge; it is the
> ability to tell right from wrong, beautiful from ugly. And this, at the rare mo-
> ments when the stakes are on the table, may indeed prevent catastrophes.[3]

As already noted, such "judging" is what is meant by the root word for
crisis and *critical*. Critical thought depends on a deep discernment that
leads to unprecedented reflection and unparalleled decisions. It is the
key, henceforth, to averting "catastrophes." Eichmann committed un-
speakable atrocities and contributed to what remains today the greatest
modern human catastrophe, so far as Arendt was concerned, because
he was capable only of conventional reasoning. He knew from his
German public-school education that one was supposed to do a good

job, obey one's superiors and provide for one's family. His argument at the trial was that he was doing everything he was expected to do under the circumstances (the so-called Nuremberg defense) and it was not his business, or even his right, to ask questions about the implications of conducting his duties, let alone act on conscience to resist it.

For all the scorn heaped on Arendt for contending that this defense made sense, today in hindsight—after all, the horrors of the Holocaust were much fresher and more shocking in the minds of her contemporaries a half century ago—we have to take it seriously. For is not rampant "political correctness," as well as the kind of automated thought processes that go into the making of today's ever-consuming political partisanship and ideology-saturated contempt and incivility toward each other in Western culture, a disturbing exemplification of everything Arendt had in mind? Arendt's point is that we can easily misread the Nazi horrors and the global "catastrophe" they wrought as something totally unique and unrepeatable in history, but in truth it was simply something that was bound to happen under exactly the right conditions, and could indeed be played out again in the future. The suppression of the critical perspective, whether by totalitarian propaganda or the insidious type of self-censorship that putatively democratic societies in any era tend to inflict on themselves (as Alexis de Tocqueville warned in the early nineteenth century), is always the occasion for catastrophe.

One of the more persistent criticisms of Arendt to which we might give some credence, nonetheless, is that her rhetoric about the "winds of thought" harbored a certain covert prejudice that "critical" awareness is reserved primarily for trained intellectuals. It is not obvious from her body of work and literary remains that she herself shared such a view, but the objection has to be considered. Even the far-seeing judgments of philosophers who, like Socrates, have been brought to trial by fire, everyday forms of ethical commitment and the moral commonplaces of their societies depend on a certain cultural context that can be neither ignored nor escaped. Any "critical" standpoint, these days, is inseparable from the context in which we find ourselves.

CRITICAL THEOLOGY AND THE SHIFTING CONTEXT

But the context itself has shifted in recent years. Until the end of the 1980s, the denouement of international Communism, and the rise of what we now term the "developing world," the "crisis" encountered by any style of critical thinking, or theorizing, was located somewhere in the collective mind of the West. Now the context has been globalized. Critical thought must always be worked through within a broader, *global* frame of reference. The question of what it means to think "globally" itself is an occasion for critical thinking. But until now the emergence of such a global critical perspective has been held back by the persistence of grand narratives concerning the meaning and purpose of history that both provide significance for our individual incentives and behavior. Such narratives routinely serve as a kind of *universal normativity* that "judges" our decisions in terms of some overarching scheme of causation and enduring value. To date, we in the West have largely been under the sway of three grand narratives—the Christian, the Marxist and the secular liberal variant of the same.

The Christian narrative, of course, is the oldest. It can be found (if we truly appreciate the metaphorical brilliance of the New Testament authors) in the efforts of the early Christian community to reinterpret the "salvation history" of their Jewish forebears in light of what Rudolf Bultmann termed the "Christ event." It comes to its theological consummation in the work of the Christian historiographer Eusebius, who reveled in the providential role of the Roman emperor Constantine in recognizing the church and legitimating it as the official religion of the empire. And it finds its enduring expression, paradoxically, a century later in the work of St. Augustine, who, writing in his *City of God,* following the sacking of Rome, the "eternal city," by the Goths, reconceives the narrative itself as the hidden hand of a mysterious God for whom the visible church becomes a crucial placeholder in the run-up to a final, cosmic, transformational event that will usher in the new heavens and new earth.

Both Marxism, as Ola Sigurdson has implied,[4] and secular liberalism, as Mark Lilla has incisively argued,[5] are latter-day, secular derivatives of the Christian grand narrative. Both bear within themselves a certain "eschatology" that construes the traditional Christian emphasis on the new *freedom in Christ* as radical freedom in a this-worldly sense. For classic liberalism, this freedom has consisted in the right to one's own life, liberty and property as well as deliverance from state interference in the economy. For Marxism, it has resided in the emancipation of the working classes from the dominion of capital as well as from the forced expropriation of their "labor power" by the machinery of capitalism. All three grand narratives embody a "providential" view of history that might be even called *predestinarian* in a certain manner of speaking, inasmuch as it singles out one who is marked for special favor—the "elect" of God," the entrepreneur, the proletariat—to perform a decisive historical role. Comprehending this special role requires an equally special "sight," a gift for critical intelligence and discernment, conferred on the elect. Finally, each variant of such a grand narrative represents a distinctive approach toward the crisis moments and trajectories of one's era. The trick is to identify the most "thought-provoking" aspects of the crisis and to grapple with them with uncompromising discipline and honesty.

The mission, therefore, of a *critical theology,* is to be able to rehabilitate the Christian narrative in a manner that both affirms its status as historically situated divine revelation and addresses decisively from a singular angle of vision the global crises in which we find ourselves enmeshed today. Such a critical theology does not shrink from the challenge of *critical thought* in its myriad philosophical, political, social, cultural and historical iterations along with its surprising, era-to-era provocations. In fact, it draws deeply on such thought in the same way a respirator forces oxygen and fresh air into a contaminated breathing environment. A critical theology cannot simply rely, as the Protestant evangelical impulse has done for centuries, on the self-evidence of the biblical "Word," which amid the clatter and clangor of an increasingly illegible contemporary history and a cacophony of alternative readings and interpretations, as well as various nonscriptural "religious" perspectives, has retreated into pure dogma and fundamentalism. The critical dimension of thought itself is the very wedge by which a critical strategy of theological thinking can take form.

At the same time, what makes critical theology distinctly *theological* and not merely a more sophisticated and penetrating mode of thought alone is its reliance on the *force of thought* that drives thought and is not reducible to the manifest elements of thought. Elsewhere I have termed this insuperable dynamo within thought the *force of God*, a largely undetected cipher for the way in which thought itself becomes the locomotive of history and in which redemption takes place. The force of God was discovered by Hegel and is the master key of much of so-called postmodern philosophy, especially what we call "deconstruction."[6] How we recognize this force within the wider architecture of both classic Christian theology and its derivative secular narratives will be explored in subsequent chapters. We cannot comprehend this force; we can only name it, acknowledge it and testify to its effects. That testimony is what traditionally we have called "faith," on which the theological stance uniquely depends.

A critical theology henceforth would be *fides informata cogitatio*, a "faith informed by thought." Or, more precisely, *fides informata cogitatio discrimine*, faith informed by *critical thinking*. It is this factor that in Latin goes by the name *discrimine* (Greek = *kritikē*), the twenty-first-century variant of *fides quaerens intellectum* ("faith seeking understanding"), which provides the general formula for any critical theology. But before we venture forth and explore the nuances of such a proposition, we need to become more clear about what exactly we mean by "critical theory."

CRITICAL THEOLOGY AND CRITICAL THEORY

In his famous and groundbreaking essay "Traditional and Critical Theory," published in 1937 on the eve of the Second World War, Max Horkheimer laid out what he considered to be the general formula for what, in a more technical and philosophical sense, I mean by critical thought. Shadowing in the background of this essay is Horkheimer's earlier piece titled "Materialism and Metaphysics" (1933), in which he critiques the kind of scientific dogmatism that had dominated the Western mind since the end of the eighteenth century. Still in many ways a committed, orthodox Marxist in the year Hitler came to power,

Horkheimer, in 1933, was interested in challenging not so much the basic premises of materialism as its "logical positivist" manifestations in the writings of the so-called Vienna circle, a rather sizable group of like-minded philosophers such as Moritz Schlick and Rudolf Carnap, who congregated in the capital of the former Austro-Hungarian empire and elaborated the view that the only legitimate forms of knowledge are those obtained through sense experience and scientific induction.

The Vienna circle had argued as well that the sole, valid kind of "theory" is *scientific theory*, insofar as it authenticates sense knowledge with clear and consistent models of inference drawn from mathematics and formal logic. Horkheimer did not dispute that scientific inference should take precedence over other types or strategies of knowing, but he wanted to correct the positivist predilection for making such strategies a mere function of newly refined observational methods. "Theory is always more than sensibility alone, and cannot be totally reduced to sensations."[7] Rather, it is about understanding the way in which knowledge itself is conditioned by social and economic relationships, and about how what Marx as a "historical materialist" regarded as changes in the underlying "substructure" of such relationships led to the alteration of the cognitive, or ideological, "superstructure" that encompasses not only culture but also science. By the same token, a deliberate effort to alter the superstructure of thought—what in later Marxist terminology became known as "consciousness raising"—by showing their dependence on one's position in a certain socioeconomic class can result in real, historical transformation of the "material conditions." Such critical self-knowledge is the key, in this relatively classical Marxist view of things, to revolutionary, political action.

Four years later, as the menace of Nazism loomed large across Europe, Horkheimer was quickly losing confidence in the capacity of the classical Marxist approach and its manner of critiquing "bourgeois" science and philosophy. By 1937 he had begun to rehabilitate, and appreciate the importance of, what since the time of Kant had come to be known as the "transcendental" perspective. Critical theory, from its inception during the 1920s, always relied at some level on Kant's claim that transcendental norms, broadly speaking, always take precedence over empirical objects or facts on the ground.

Reeling from the disastrous legacy of National Socialism with its pernicious "racial science," the Frankfurt school appropriately grasped that allegedly "disinterested" appeals to the "data" of science could easily become a subterfuge for acts of callous inhumanity. There could be no such thing as a "value-neutral" form of objectivity, especially in a realm of investigation that had come to be considered the "social" sciences. Jürgen Habermas, however, was more conciliatory to the social sciences, particularly as a relatively young scholar during the 1970s. He did not cling to the touchstone of transcendental normativity, as had most of the Frankfurt school up through Marcuse, but relied more on the other facet of Kantian philosophy, that is, the contention that rationality itself has its limits and cannot go beyond what the British philosopher Peter Strawson called the "bounds of sense."[8] Habermas therefore, early on, took much the same tack as the American pragmatist philosopher Richard Rorty in arguing that conventional liberalism should be preferred over dogmatic Marxism because it realizes the fallible nature of all thought and action. His "critique" of existing society differed measurably from the former Frankfurt school to the extent that he perceived certain virtues in the "freedom" afforded by liberal democracy and its built-in checks against runaway totalitarianism. But Habermas was still searching for a distinctive "critical" edge that might have the force of the dialectic apart from the dialectic itself. As it turned out, he discovered that critical angle of vision neither in Hegelianism nor in Marxism, but in the philosophy of language.

Relatively early in his career, Habermas read the writings of the so-called speech-act theorists—British philosophers such as J. L. Austin and John Searle who touted their ideas from the late 1950s onward. Speech-act theory served to redirect the philosophy of language during the latter quarter of the twentieth century in both the Anglophone academy and on the Continent, and it had an impressive follow-on through the writings of Jacques Derrida and the "post-structuralists." Speech-act theory, inspired by the earlier work of Ludwig Wittgenstein and his dictum of "meaning as use," is most notable for shifting the focus of philosophical inquiry from an analysis of propositions and the practices of predicative logic to what might be referred to as the "rhetorical" function of language, that is, the "pragmatic" role of linguistic operations and means of communication.

In his 1955 lectures at Harvard University titled "How to Do Things with Words," Austin argued that hitherto philosophy had been baffled by types of expression that do not count straightforwardly as "statements" and thus could not apply the usual criteria of "evidence" or "verifiability" to them. The outlier, persistently ignored by the prevailing philosophy of the era, consisted in a unique "locutionary" act where "the uttering of the sentence is, or is a part of, the doing of an action, which again would not normally be described as saying something."[9] Such all-too-familiar and ubiquitous means of expression—for example, threats, commands, predictions or promise making—are to be judged as to their validity in terms of their effects or outcomes, not the "logical" values normally derived from carrying out a predicative calculus.

What at the time consisted in a genuinely revolutionary perspective on what language really is and how it works prompted Habermas to reconsider the models of human action—and *interaction*—that had earlier prevailed in both Marxist philosophy and the newer ventures of critical theory. Whereas previous "materialist" paradigms had stressed the collective and at times mechanical nature of historical change and human solidarity, Habermas zeroed in on the way in which intersubjective relations, together with the routine employment of what the famed scholar Noam Chomsky had dubbed "linguistic competence," might be considered the key to what the critical theorists envisioned as the "rational society." In earlier iterations of critical theory, the notion of a rational society turned on sophisticated assessments of the structures of domination and the ideological systems that, as Marx had propounded, mask systematic distortions of everyday human relationships. However, in his two-volume *magnum opus* titled *The Theory of Communicative Action*, which first appeared in the mid-1980s, Habermas moved from the kind

of *macro-theoretical* critiques that characterized the work of his predecessors to a new strategy of *micro-analysis* concerning how the social
body is disfigured through misformed constellations of discourse and
how these configurations, identified in the past as structures of "alienation," can be repaired through a refurbishing of democracy based on
new kinds of linguistic strategies.

HABERMAS AND THE RELIGIOUS FACTOR

In articulating this general theory of "communicative action" and the
mode of "communicative rationality" that Habermas believed it was necessary to nurture if the emancipatory potential of critical theory were to
ultimately be realized, he reached back anew into the nineteenth century
and drew appreciably on the work of Max Weber as well as Marx. Habermas
cited Weber's "teleological," as opposed to a mechanistic, prototype of
human conduct and noted that all knowledge has a certain "interest" in
being shared as well as acknowledged and accepted by other social actors.
What makes these interests "rational" is not so much their conformance
with some all-encompassing explanatory or "scientific" model, but the fact
that they can be formulated in language and their linguistic tokens deployed to reach certain mutually agreeable as well as intelligible endpoints.
In other words, society thrives on reciprocal understanding along with the
art of negotiation and persuasion. "An agent can either pursue his own
interests, such as acquiring power or wealth," Habermas writes, "or he can
attempt to live up to values such as piety or human dignity, or he can seek
satisfaction in living out affects and desires."[10] Figuring out how people can
"live up" to such "values," and detailing the kinds of structures required to
have them do so, is where the rubber literally meets the road when it comes
critical theory. In the *Theory of Communicative Action,* Habermas also
drew a distinction between what he labeled "system" and "life world." The
system is the greater infrastructure of society that can be regarded as "rational" only in the measure that it supports the rationality of communicative action itself within the "life world," hence bolstering the ability of
participants in a democracy to work out their differences and to find a

common public "space" within which they can express, frame and mediate each other's predilections and interests.

Habermas's theory of communicative action was challenged from the outset by representatives of two important and influential intellectual communities, the Marxist and the Christian. The Marxists tended to see the theory of communicative action as a betrayal of the hard critique of bourgeois culture and society that the Frankfurt school especially had been so deft in redesigning and updating to go along with the times. In fact, Habermas's tendency to advocate for "cosmopolitanism" and "post-modern" forms of democratic capitalism, as we find enshrined nowadays in the laws and institutions of the European Union, prompted some of his critics to claim he had defected from his Marxist heritage altogether. At the same time, many Christian theologians, or religious theorists, were apt to fault what appeared to be Habermas's utter lack of attention to faith commitments and faith-based strands of discourse in the kinds of public give-and-take and value positions that any empirical sociologist would be forced to acknowledge as figuring heavily in the formation of the "life world." The public square is "naked," these critics asserted, without religion. The language of religion is as much an element of the "communicative" practices of democracy as secular conversations.

Around the turn of the millennium, and especially after the trauma of September 11, 2001, Habermas began to vigorously identify religion as an important sociopolitical player and as a necessary ingredient in the discourse of democracy. The election of a German pope with a mission to revive an appreciation for the "Christian" character of Europe was another factor as well, especially as it affected Habermas's magisterial role as an intellectual voice for the fledgling European Union. In a dialogue with Pope Benedict XVI (formerly Cardinal Joseph Ratzinger) Habermas insisted that any "solidarity" among peoples and individuals in a liberal democracy demands shared norms of discourse for framing issues and mediating differences. Rather than excluding religion from this arena of communicative reason, both philosophers and political thinkers should welcome it, so long as it sees itself not as having the final say or adhering to nonnegotiable positions, even if the latter arise from unqualified faith convictions. Instead, both religious and secular parties must agree to restrict the scope of their claims, even while both sides can benefit from engagement with each other. "We should understand cultural and societal secularization," Habermas writes, "as a double learning process that compels both the traditions of the Enlightenment and the religious doctrines to reflect on their own respective limits."[11] This solution of social rationality as self-limitation can be traced back to the political writings of Kant. At the same time, Kant understood faith as a form of pure *moral* normativity that accepted unconditional constraints on any claim to supernatural insight or supernatural truth (what he dubbed "religion within the limits of reason alone"), whereas Habermas has insisted all along that communicative action requires secular rationality itself to recognize and acquiesce to its own limitations. "With regard to post-secular societies, we must ask which cognitive attitudes and normative expectations the liberal state must require its citizens—both believers and unbelievers—to put into practice in their dealings with each other."[12]

However, it is not simply a matter, Habermas insists, of religious people and secular people learning to "get along" and to communicate effectively with each other. The ideals of the Enlightenment cannot simply ignore the Western legacy of "revealed knowledge," which has forged and shaped its mission. As Habermas writes well into his later career,

> If religious and metaphysical worldviews prompted similar learning processes, then both modes, faith and knowledge, together with their traditions based respectively in Jerusalem and Athens, belong to the history of the origins of the secular reason which today provides the medium in which the sons and daughters of modernity communicate concerning their place in the world.[13]

If there is anything we can say about the grand Habermasian project, it can be described as an effort to reclaim the dignity and sovereign prerogative of rationality as uncompromising *logos*, as inaugurated by the Greeks. Indeed, this effort summarizes in many respects the goals and aims of critical theory as a whole. However, Habermas is clearly ambivalent when it comes to allowing religion to share in a new global enterprise of "shared reason." He suggests that the West currently is in a "process of de-Hellenization" as a consequence of globalization, a claim that seems intuitively correct.

At the same time, Habermas views this process as retrogressive rather than emancipatory. The "resurgence" of religion "is going hand-in-hand with an increase in the frequency of conflicts between different religious groups and denominations. Even though many of these conflicts have different origins, they become inflamed when they are codified in religious terms."[14] We have now restored at a global level the historical conditions of the seventeenth century. What Derrida dubbed the "return of religion" actually amounts to a set of new planetary "wars of religion." Habermas proposes that the "neutrality" of the liberal state when it comes to religion is even more crucial now than it was several centuries ago, insofar as the state's capacity to pacify the conflict is at once necessary to nurturing the circumstances under which a new kind of truly universal *logos* might eventually flourish.

The task of a critical theology would be to ask the kind of question posed by the elder Habermas—namely, can there be a universal *logos* with the "critical" function that both the original instantiations of critical theory and "crisis theology" set forth? In order to begin to frame a response to such a question, we need first to consider the relationship between the political formations through which the interests of "secular reason" instantiate themselves and the "theological" dimensions that inevitably intrude into these kinds of arrangements. In other words, we must ask about the relationship between critical theology and what is more familiarly understood as "political theology."

3

From Political Theology to a
Global Critical Theology

Those who say religion has nothing to do with
politics do not know what religion is.

MAHATMA GANDHI

THE MEANING OF POLITICAL THEOLOGY

What do we mean by political theology? The late Jewish religious philosopher Jacob Taubes, one of the progenitors of the field of political theology, has put the matter as follows: "In the beginning theology emerged as a problem of political theory."[1] To inquire about the nature of political theology, it is first imperative that we ask ourselves exactly what we mean by theology, according to Taubes, and in making this move we discover that theology was intimately bound up with the political from the very beginning.

The term *theology* first appears in Plato's *Republic*. The *Republic* itself consists of a dialogue that explores the interlinkages between the concept of "justice" (*dikaiosynē*) and the makeup of the *polis*, or city-state. In the dialogue Plato seeks to come to terms with the genuine nature of the "gods" (*theoi*), who traditionally have been called on to guarantee social and political order. Taubes argues that the idea of "theology" derives from the crisis of the Greek cities, corresponding to the "twilight of the Olympian gods" and "the end of Greek society." The end of the gods, therefore, was the inauguration of theological inquiry. "The issue of theology was for Plato intrinsically related to political theory," Taubes writes, and hence, "there is, in fact, no theology that should not be relevant for the order of society. Even a theology that claims to be apolitical altogether, and conceives the divine as the totally foreign, as the totally other to man and world, may have political implications." In the same manner that theology is essentially bound up with the political, the political is inseparable from, and is historically conditioned by, the theological. Finally, "as there is no theology without political implications, there is no political theory without theological presuppositions."[2] In the end, the two spheres share more in common than is supposed, and perhaps hoped for.

At the same time, Taubes did not successfully answer the question of *how* the theological and the political—at least thematically—enmesh with each other. Nor did Taubes seriously account for the multifarious uses of the term that had already come into circulation over the last three-quarters century when he made this observation. Indeed, the expression *political theology* was first given serious currency in the present era by the German jurist Carl Schmitt during the German Weimar era, when both crisis theology and critical theory were in gestation. Schmitt, a profoundly committed Roman Catholic thinker, was at the same time standing with both feet in a tradition that goes back many centuries before.

Throughout this tradition we can find no dominant and all-sufficient definition of political theology that makes sense, other than the inchoate notion that theological thinking must somehow have a specific relevance to the broader realm of public affairs. In recent years, the word has come to have an expansive range of connotations. As far as Adam Kotsko is concerned, "the field of political theology has not yet been rigorously defined. It is more a field of affinities than a clearly delineated disciplinary space—a kind of 'zone of indistinction' between theology and political theory where the terms of debate are still very much up for grabs."[3] Elsewhere Creston Davis notes that "it is true that the subject of political theology resists singular definition; indeed the term functions like a nebulous concept—a Rorschach test whose ink markings are given meaning by the individual perceiver taking the exam."[4] We can naturally generate many possible definitions of political theology in the same fashion that we can come up with different methods and approaches, both to situate the problem theoretically, and to offer different strategies of explication and application. We are irresistibly wedded to a multitude of different perspectives and procedures.

The necessity of adopting a "pluralist" stance when it comes to political theology nowadays arises from the fact that we live in a world of diverse cultures, philosophical legacies, habits of reasoning and moral and religious frameworks within which traditional intellectual problems are now addressed. Political theology was once upon a time a distinctive form of Christian discourse. It has become grist in recent years for discussions and debates within many diverse religious communities and even among those who have no clearly etched religious, or theological, identity. It is, therefore, incumbent on us to examine the context and specific content of those various writings as well as the motivations of those exemplary figures associated with the idea of a political theology.

One of the key distinctions around which so much of contemporary discourse about political theology revolves is Claude Lefort's differentiation between the theory of the political (*la politique*) and the realm of politics (*le politique*).[5] Though Lefort does not traffic to any degree in the locution *political theology* per se, political theology traverses both sides of the boundary he draws. Political theology can be construed as a type of reflection on the "metaphysical" or more abstruse facets of the political, or it may have to do with the analysis of present-day politics, or it may constitute an examination of both the theoretical and practical at the same time. Furthermore, we can partition off, Lefort implies, what we know as "political theology" into two more technicalities: the *theopolitical* and *political religions*. The first approach touches on the subjects of philosophy and ethics, whereas *political religions* are concerned with *le politique*; that is, they investigation the social-scientific and historical dimensions of religion and its relation to political life.

Both approaches can be subsumed under the broader idiom of political theology. However, political theology in the more restricted sense tends to resist the idea of a neutral or "objective" investigation of religious phenomena (what in the nineteenth century was known by the German word *Religionswissenschaft*, or "science of religion"). Because it has been preoccupied ever since Plato with finding normative principles by which political life can be configured, political theology classically has cared little for what historical research tells us about the way in which religion works in practice. In addition, political theology habitually has had little to do with the now established academic field, especially in the Anglo-American world, of so-called religious studies, the multimethodological consideration of anything that might be called "religious," past and present.

Religious studies scholars conventionally look at religion in its functional, pragmatic or purely sociocultural roles and do not ask the kind of deeper, theoretical questions that theology historically has always posed, a point I have driven home in many of my own writings.[6] When it comes to the "political" side of religion, the very same theorists—especially since the eighteenth century—have been accustomed to explaining away religious belief and practice as nothing more than a device used by those in power to control the masses.

THE HISTORICAL MEANING OF *POLITICAL THEOLOGY*

What have we meant by *political theology* historically? The term *political theology* itself first occurs in the literature of ancient Rome, particularly that of the Stoic philosophers. The first mention is with Marcus Terentius Varro (116–27 BCE).[7] Varro's actual writings have been lost, but his *Antiquities* are cited regularly among the church fathers. In *Antiquities*, Varro, a so-called civic theologian who was the famous foil for St. Augustine in his attack on paganism in the opening chapters of his *City of God*, lays out a triple division (*theologia tripartia)* of "natural theology" (*cosmikē, naturalis*), "mythic theology" (*mythikē, fabularis*) and "political theology" (*politikē, civilis*).[8] Natural theology encompasses speculation by the philosophers of Greco-Roman times. Mythic theology refers to the popular worldviews promoted by poets and playwrights. Political theology signifies the literary productions of the priests of the "civil religion" of ancient Rome. If we could imagine a field devoted exclusively to the compilation and dissemination of the writings and speeches of chaplains, politicians and public pastoral figures like Billy Graham when they are commenting on matters of national interest, it would come close to what Varro had in mind for his own age.

Following Augustine's repudiation of Varro, the word *political theology* vanishes in the West's lexicon, but resurfaces in the work of Baruch Spinoza, a seventeenth-century Jewish philosopher who exerted a tremendous influence on the Enlightenment, or the so-called Age of Reason, a hundred years later. The work in question is Spinoza's *Theologico-Political Treatise*, published in 1677 after his death. The treatise as a whole centers on the struggle between faith and reason, or between the authority of religious revelation and philosophical inquiry unassisted by theological assumptions. As the famous twentieth-century political philosopher Leo Strauss has written, "The chief aim of the *Treatise* is to refute claims which had been raised on behalf of revelation throughout the ages; and Spinoza succeeded, at least to the extent that his book has become *the* classic document of the 'rationalist' or 'secularist' attack on the belief in revelation."[9]

Strauss sees Spinoza as having reframed the question of the connection between the theological and the political in such stark terms that conventional "secular" thinking since his time has forced us without warrant to choose between the two terms. However, Strauss has suggested that Spinoza inadvertently compelled us no longer to see the political as simply derived from the theological, but as a handmaiden to it. Strauss's main focus itself turned out to be the problem of what Lefort calls the "theological-political," that is, the deployment of theological aims and presuppositions to resolve political questions. In Strauss's mind, the dilemma amounted to that implied in the church father Tertullian's famous question: "What does Athens have to do with Jerusalem?" In other words, for which authority should we opt—that of God and his divine revelation, or human beings and their reliance on the natural

powers of reason and critical discernment? For Strauss, political theology "is about the theological ordering of human affairs, and about the
ordering of human affairs on the basis of revealed religion as a practice."[10]

The next major figure to utilize the notion of political theology is
Schmitt himself, who is famous for the following statement:

> All significant concepts of the modern theory of the state are secularized theo-
> logical concepts not only because of their historical development—in which
> they are transferred from theology to the theory of the state, whereby for
> example, the omnipotent God became the omnipotent law giver—but also
> because of their systematic structure, the recognition of which is necessary
> for a sociological consideration of these steps.[11]

Hence, the political becomes its own form of a substitute, secularized religion strutting on the stage after the demise of Western Christendom.
Schmitt's statement anticipates the views of the present-day French political
and religious theorist Olivier Roy, who writes that "secularization does not
mean the end of transcendence but the establishment of a nontheological
transcendence, in a sense of a secularized religion."[12] Roy's "secularized
religion" would be the same as the modern swearing of allegiance to the
nation-state, a kind of religiosity the turn-of-the-century French sociologist
Émile Durkheim regarded as the essence of religion itself.[13]

British philosopher Roger Scruton characterizes political theology in
much the same manner. It is, he says,

> the transfer of theological concepts to the political sphere, emphasizing man's
> fallen character, the defect of original sin, and the need for an authoritative
> legal order that would do justice to the longing for redemption. Political The-
> ology can be discerned in the writings of Rousseau and Hegel, both of whom
> are given to describing the political reality in terms borrowed from Christian
> theology, and in the writings of many Russian political thinkers.[14]

Banu Bargu further notes that

> secularization does not lead to the progressive disappearance of the theo-
> logical; on the contrary, the theological always leaves its trace in the structure
> of the secular, and this trace has a determining quality. On the one hand, the
> theological is written into the secular, becoming a latent participant in its

meaning connotations, and implications. On the other, the sacred and the secular co-exist in the self-consciousness of an era that, in turn, fashions the political after its own image.[15]

Political theology is therefore, for Bargu, a kind of theory of secularization, which seeks to locate the sacred within the secular life of society, as it puts its political ideas into practice.

Political theology unmasks the pretensions of everyday political thought either by identifying the covert ways in which religious ideas are smuggled into the very grammar of politics or by showing how many presumed "secular" ideas happen to be religious or theological views in disguise. At minimum, many political ideas have their own theological genealogy, as the contemporary political thinker Mark Lilla has argued: "Many of our contemporary basic principles—human rights, toleration, even the religious-secular distinction—have roots in Christian theology and canon law."[16] At the same time, political theology demonstrates how the sacred lurks behind many supposedly pure political notions. We find such notions in the familiar ideal, shared by nations the world over for ages, of the sacrifice of the individual for the motherland or the fatherland. Philosopher Paul Kahn has argued in his *Political Theology: Four New Chapters on the Concept of Sovereignty* that the American "political imaginary" is shot through with an admiration for sacrificial violence, since so many American documents, including the Constitution, are contextualized in terms of the violence and suffering of American patriots during the Revolutionary War.[17]

A further illustration of the interpenetration of the sacred with the secular can be found in the ideology and propaganda of Hitler's Third Reich. Michael Hoelzl writes in his preface to Rainer Bucher's *Hitler's Theology: A Study in Political Religion* that

> Hitler's political project gains power by drawing on religious ideas and reinterpreting them in his own theological way. Central to Hitler's project are the idea of community (*völkische Gemeinschaft*) and providence (*Vorsehung*) as legitimation of his role as the chosen leader. Given these two aspects of Christian theology, it would be more accurate to rephrase Schmitt's thesis with respect to Hitler's theology: All significant concepts of Hitler's modern theory of the "state" are secularized and bastardized theological concepts.[18]

CARL SCHMITT AND CONTEMPORARY CONNOTATIONS

Schmitt is without question the architect of modern political theology, who remains to this day the "gray eminence" whose portrait peers over a convoluted legacy that has arisen from his original writings in the 1920s. On the other hand, political theology's ascent as a recognized, and recognizable, academic discipline in the sense with which we are currently familiar starts in Germany during the 1960s with the writings of Johann Baptist Metz, Jürgen Moltmann and Dorothee Soelle. These religious thinkers altogether were confronted with the question of how Nazism was able to gain such a stronghold, and to possess the minds and morals of a would-be "Christian" country. They asked why the church had been silent and indifferent, barring a few key exceptions such as the followers of Barth, over the persecution of Jews, and had turned a blind eye to the Holocaust. What kind of God allowed the Holocaust to happen? they asked.

Religious philosopher Michael Hoelzl finds that "political theology stands for a certain school of Christian theology and has its roots in Catholicism."[19] Such a political theology is an heir to the liberalization of the Catholic Church that accompanied Vatican II and inspired the young theologian Johann Baptist Metz. Metz was the kind of Catholic thinker whose own "theopolitics" was stalked by "the attempt to escape the shadow of Carl Schmitt."[20] For Hoelzl, we can figure out generally what Metz means by "political theology" by quoting the theologian himself: "Political theology has many meanings and is therefore open to misunderstandings. Furthermore, the term is historically problematic." Nevertheless, it can be characterized intrinsically as follows: "*The deprivatizing of theology is the primary critical task of political theology.*"[21] Such a theology counts as "a critical correction of present-day theology inasmuch as this theology shows an extreme privatizing tendency (a tendency, that is, to center on the private person, rather than 'public,' 'political' society). At the same time," Metz insists, "I understand this political theology to be a positive attempt to formulate the eschatological message under the conditions of our present society."[22] Metz, at the time, was thinking of the privatized religion and moralistic values of bourgeois Christianity in

Europe, the same kind of self-satisfied, institutionalized brand of religiosity that Kierkegaard targeted in the mid-nineteenth century. In Metz's understanding, political theology is to constitute an "eschatologically" sensitive community that bears within itself the "dangerous memory" of the death and resurrection of Jesus Christ.

In a groundbreaking essay that appeared in *Theology Today* in the early 1970s, Moltmann, Metz's academic contemporary, offered a new take on political theology.

> Political theology is therefore not simply political ethics, but reaches further by asking about the political consciousness of theology itself. It does not want to make political questions the central theme of theology or to give political systems and movements religious support. Rather, political theology designates the field, the milieu, the environment, and the medium in which Christian theology should be articulated today. Political theology is therefore a hermeneutical category.[23]

The notion of political theology as a "hermeneutics," or theory of interpretation, is both radical and provocative, and it speaks to how to begin to shape the relationship between political theology and what I am terming "critical theology." According to Moltmann, this hermeneutical understanding of theology that distinguishes political theology can only be derived from the very linchpin of Christian faith itself, the cross. "The cross is the point at which Christian faith distinguishes itself from other religion and ideologies, from unfaith and superstition. It is worthy of note that the cross of Christ is also the only true political point in the story of Jesus. It should therefore become the beginning point and the criterion for a Christian political theology."[24]

Moltmann's impact on European and American theological thought was immense for at least two decades, from the early 1970s onward. The kind of "hermeneutical" theology he pioneered laid the groundwork for the emergence of the highly influential movement known as "liberation theology," founded by Peruvian priest Gustavo Gutiérrez. Gutiérrez's now well-known dictum that theology should exhibit a "preferential option for the poor," drawn from his own ethnic identity as a Peruvian

Indian, and his extensive experience as a Dominican friar with the plight
of the marginalized and impoverished in the slums of Lima, can be considered a radical and applied version of Moltmann's theme of the "crucified God." Christianity's crucified God signals that God is against the
high and mighty and in favor of the outcast and dispossessed, in the
raising of all of the world's *nonpersons* into the realm of human dignity
and historical life.

The specific social and political emphases of liberation theology as it
developed in the last part of the twentieth century made some of its conservative critics wonder whether it was not merely secular leftist politics
with a theological veneer. Pope John Paul II, the Polish prelate who as
pontiff was celebrated for his resistance to Soviet Communism, was instrumental in the effort to suppress and eventually censor outright the liberation theologians within the Catholic faith community because of their
not-so-subtle association of the gospel with Marxist philosophy. Gutiérrez
himself was investigated as a heretic (though he was never formally cen-
sured) until the inauguration of Pope Francis, who perhaps because of his
own South American background immediately rehabilitated the founder
of liberation theology. But it is this very obvious and *very real* political edge
to "political theology" that has made it an increasingly influential force
shaping the contemporary order of things.

With the advent of globalization we are now compelled to examine both
intelligently and concretely the social, economic and political intercon-
nections at a transparently international level among peoples, institutions
and events. Political theology, no matter its "liberal" or "conservative"
slant, is inextricably caught up in media res, in the messy midst of things.
It can no longer be regarded simply as a kind of "politicized" excursus into
daily affairs that is still conducted from the pulpit or within the academy
and relies on the canonized wisdom of those intellectual giants who have
preceded us.

One of the fundamental issue of political theology nowadays is how
"theological" inquiry takes account of the "religious" factor in its global
and multifaith manifestations, especially when what exactly we mean by

"religion" can no longer be answered through appeal to classical Christian assumptions. As Graham Hammill and Julia Reinhard Lupton have noted, political theology does not take the "religious," whatever is implied in that expression, for granted at all. They insist that "political theology is not the same as religion.

> Instead, we take it to name a form of questioning that arises precisely when religion is no longer a dominant explanatory or life mode. Political theology reflects and feeds on a crisis in religion, whether that crisis is understood historically (as Reformation) or existentially (as doubt, skepticism or boredom).[25]

In the current era, political theology has morphed from its earlier preoccupations with issues of sovereignty and secularity to an effort to come to terms with the new postmodern and post-secular set of conditions under which we live in this age of globalization. The slate of questions about the connection between the political and theological that were raised in the eras of antiquity, modernity and most of the twentieth century have now been wiped clean, and a new constellation of problems, quandaries and range of solutions is becoming slowly visible. Taking this altered environment into account, Michael Kessler makes the case that political theology must reshape itself as a comparative venture. He also notes that political theology must refashion itself as *both* a descriptive methodology that "apprehends, catalogs, and analyzes empirical political phenomenon . . . and a constructive enterprise in which theory is developed and critically applied in . . . prescriptive statements about the way politics ought to be configured."[26]

A similar take can be found in the writings of scholars such as Elizabeth Phillips, who is convinced that political theology, as part of a new global ecumenism, must be relativized and pursue diverse "trajectories" in accordance with the theological pluralism of the world religions.[27] Finally, noted philosopher of religion Hent de Vries offers a cognate assessment in writing that "political theology" provides survey and analysis of the "ever-changing relationships between political community and religious order, in short, between power and salvation."[28]

POLITICAL THEOLOGY AND CULTURAL PLURALISM

The attempt to synchronize the agenda of political theology with the fact of cultural pluralism has been an ongoing project at different levels and with different ends in view over the past half century. But what if pluralism itself were an outdated frame of reference coinciding with the prevalence of the so-called neoliberal economic world order that is now unraveling? What if Derrida's "return of religion," a return we now are witnessing full-blown in the explosion around the globe of radical Islamism, signified an era of "post-secularism," as it has been called, that feeds off the appeal of religion not as a private faith option in a liberal social order that tolerates most every option, but as a force that challenges and seeks with militant fervor to transform the order as a whole?

That is basically the argument of British theologian Graham Ward, who equates the return of religion with the twilight of the postmodern age. According to Ward, postmodernity was always coincident with the rise of global capitalism. But since the worldwide financial debacle of 2008, the slow deflation of the global economy has meant that the sort of happy multiculturalism, as well as the moral relativism and experimentalism that characterized so much of the postmodern ethos, has lost its luster. The return of religion corresponds to the growing human desire to take life more seriously, to confront the chaotic conditions of the world we see around us and to take a stand in decisive instances. The lure of political theology is that it can combine the ethical need for making value judgments based on what are frequently recognized as transcendental principles with an understanding that political life is always about real choices.

In Ward's view what is absolutely indispensible to politics is the willingness to pass judgment. Here Ward builds on a modified version of Schmitt's notion that politics is all about making decisions following from what he calls the "friend/enemy" distinction. Incorporating what has been called Schmitt's "decisionism" in the formulation of the task of political theology, Ward writes, "There is a need for the passing of judgment before there can be a determination of the friend, the enemy, and the distinction between them." The axiom that politics rests on the will of that person, or collective persona, to make judgments and render decisions, suffuses the very marrow of political theology.

> But all political theology can be conceived as the formation and passing of judgment; where judgment has numerous gradations from offering critique, constructing an argument for or an argument against, championing the oppressed and the marginalized, championing the oppressed and the marginalized, and propounding an alternative perspective to the declarations of the enemy and the amassing of friends for a fight.[29]

Christian political theology, for Ward (and he strongly implies there really is no other kind of political theology), takes Scripture as the ongoing context for making judgments, especially when it comes to social ethics and a determination of the proper relationship between rules and the ruled, or between oppressors and the oppressed. In fact, the biblical scholar Walter Brueggemann, insists that the strong moral and prophetic tone common to the legacy of Western political theology can be attributed directly to its biblical sources.

> The self-presentation of Israel in song and story is inescapably a *theological politics* in which the defining presence of YHWH, the God of Israel, impinges upon every facet of the political; or conversely, Israel's self representation is inescapably a *political theology* in which YHWH, the God of Israel, is intensely engaged with questions of power and with policies and practices that variously concern the distribution of goods and access. In Israel's self representation, there is no politics not theologically marked, no theology not politically inclined.[30]

Thus political theology makes compelling moral claims and carries with it, as Lilla has made clear, the unmistakable imprint of biblical revelation, which grounds both the assumptions and the commitments of much of Western political economy overall.

When all is said and done, political theology is a by-product of the centuries-long puzzle and debate within the West over the appropriate interrelationships between the secular and the religious. What Lilla refers to as the "Great Separation" that got underway in Europe during the seventeenth century between the political and the theological, or between the authority of religion and the power of the state, has been all along the framework for the elaboration of what we know as political theology. Political theology is neither an aide-de-camp for theology, insofar as it strives to place religious constraints on the state apparatus, nor does it merely play a conciliatory role in endeavoring to make secular political norms and requirements congenial to the theological mind as a whole. Political theology straddles the post-Reformation divide between the secular and the religious, even if we are indeed entering a "post-secular" time, as Ward suggests. Thus the historic uncoupling of the two spheres— what Martin Luther regarded as the "two kingdoms" in which we all enjoy dual citizenship—has made political theology an urgent necessity, even when we contend with cultures and societies such as Islamic ones that do not historically recognize the relevance of the distinction.

Recent terrorist attacks by radical Islamists underscore how the struggle between the hegemony of the sacred versus that of the secular may have largely subsided in the democracies of the West. But it has now become a fierce bone of contention in the new and mounting struggle between what the late political philosopher Samuel Huntington dubbed "the West and the rest." In the words of Dimitris Vardoulakis, "Political theology refers to the impossibility of both to completely separate and to completely conflate politics and religion. And as Kenneth Reinhard stresses, 'the political order is sustained by theological concepts that it cannot completely assimilate.'"[31]

The Great Separation itself may be considered a product of the modern Western imaginary, in which reason and revelation are kept in separate, airtight boxes and at a convenient distance from each other. Reason governs the affairs of human beings according to this outlook, and hence of an entirely worldly politics, where religious priorities are regarded as merely one factional claim among many possible ones. Rev-elation may be respected as a valid warrant for moral judgments and prescriptions (although there has always been a "strict separationist" strand of secularism, which shades from time to time into a stance of outright atheism). Yet its heavenly assurance cannot ever, and should not, impinge on what philosopher Charles Taylor has characterized as the "immanent frame" of secular society with its own laws, customs and pluralistic sensitivities.

However, it is possible to argue, in summary, that what political theology does in its encounter with secular pluralism is essentially to attribute God's demands not strictly to the private conscience of the individual, but to the domain of the political in its collective finality, even if such a transfer of authority amounts to little more than agitation that religion be allowed to compete equally for influence in the "public square." Emilio Gentile's *Politics as Religion* makes the case that the political and the religious are no longer effectively separated, because politics counts as religion nowadays and vice versa.[32]

Hence the era of "privatized" and apolitical faith that predominated throughout most of the twentieth century has quietly come to an end. Schmitt's famous, or infamous, friend/enemy distinction as the epitome of the political now pervades all aspects of politics in the West, and the much-lamented vicious "partisanship" of democratic politics, especially in America, may be accounted for as a confrontation between value systems as much as a show of personal or collective animosities.[33] Much of the value conflict has to do with different constituencies with strong, uncompromising (we might even say "metaphysical") commitments to such issues as abortion or gay rights, which may or may not have a recognizable religious origin, but definitely function as if they were based on inviolable religious truth of some sort.

Despite the operative gap between the secular and the religious, or the political and the theological, the boundary line between the two remains fluid and permeable. Political theology takes into serious account the new gray zone that encompasses the so-called two kingdoms. If the world today is undergoing what some scholars have termed a "reenchantment" (hence the denominator *post-secular*), the real reason may be, as Talal Asad has suggested in various writings, the concurrent disenchantment with the nation-state as the guarantor of secular democracy, especially in the Islamic world.[34] Economic integration, through global capitalism, driven in large part by the necessity of open borders for the free flow of money, labor and consumer expendables, as well as the explosion of the different means of digital communications, has made the centralized government of the nation-state itself increasingly ineffective and ultimately inconsequential. Political theology thus reflects this new set of circumstances.

POLITICAL THEOLOGY AND THE "RETURN" OF THE RELIGIOUS

Political theology is no longer about the part religious motivation must play within the machinery of national sovereignty. It comes down to how distinctively "religious" factors can or ought to be negotiated with the "secular" dimensions of the multinational and multipolar reality of the present. The secularity with which the religious must be negotiated, however, is one in which our global consensus, day by day, no longer is apt to interpret as the bedrock of some universal liberal (or neoliberal) order of things. On the contrary, it is regarded as a manifestation of a historic but waning European hubris that must be vigorously contested.

It is in this context of accelerating globalization, which has spawned expectations of a new and different type of world order as well as a sense of a metastasizing planetary chaos that we can begin to envision a transition from the old models of political theology, to a new vision of a *global critical theology*. A global critical theology no longer relies on Western assumptions of nationality and the historical forms of political self-definition and the criteria of sovereignty. At the same time, it is not simply an idle gesture, or genuflection, to some vague notion of political and theological multiplicity on a global scale. The whole celebrated notion of a frictionless, pluralistic world order in which peoples from the remotest corners of every continent can equally and respectfully share their distinctive social or ethnic identities and idiosyncrasies in some grand "multicultural" bazaar enabled by ever-novel advances in commerce and communication is a contemporary liberal fantasy equivalent to the hopes invested in the League of Nations in the 1920s.

A global critical theology—as we have already seen in the etymology of the term *critical*—seeks to dive into the international underworld of political turmoil and dramatic cultural change, in order to discern *both* the hidden negative, or "dialectical," factors that are inconspicuously determining present affairs *and* at the same time are harboring the hidden promise of transformation and human emancipation. A global critical theology, therefore, probes concertedly and decisively in the direction of the universal—rather than the tribal, ethnic or any other particularistic—meaning of these factors and forces that are instrumental in the reshaping of things to come.

What is becoming clear, especially in light of the incontrovertible fact of the "return of religion" as exhibited in new and aggressive forms of the "theopolitical," is that these forces and factors do not amount to the same kind of "immanent" rules of explanation that have prevailed in the secular, modern epoch. We can, of course, take the easy way out and return to the stance of dialectical theology with its pronouncement of *Nein* over everything that is the "word of man" and appeal simply, as Barth and his contemporaries did, to the presumed, self-evident truths of Christian revelation as contained in the incontrovertible "Word of God."

But the strategy of the old crisis, or dialectical, theology was based on the assumption that there remained in the current era a vital kernel throughout at least the Western world of Christian belief, self-understanding and theological conviction (the underlying premise in accordance with which Barth was able over much of his life to compose his massive, multivolume magnum opus, *Church Dogmatics*). That may have been true as late as the 1950s, but it has not been the case now for half a century. Christian thought always has its own mere "faith fallback," which can energize a committed sectarian community in the same way that so-called red meat rhetoric and sloganeering is capable of mobilizing a partisan base in electoral politics.

Such language unwittingly assumes the persistence of a certain Christian theological hegemony in the world, the vanished kingdom we remember as Christendom. Yet it is insufficient to contend with the messy confusion of combative claims and counterclaims, as well as political salvos—some still secular, many increasingly religious—that can

increasingly activate even stronger passions than what so much of the
Christian faithful these days can express. A critical theology, therefore,
has to detect and articulate the nature of the *force* behind faith. It is incumbent on such theological thinkers to realize how that force is pushing,
molding and redirecting events within the course of history.

The biblical narrative, mainly the story of the Old Testament prophets,
shows us how when faith becomes overly self-confident, comfortable in
its own private zone of religious assumptions, and hence self-deceiving,
it turns out to be idolatrous. It is the very essence of idolatry that it
cannot recognize itself as idolatrous. Idolatrous faith often has all the
right discourse and all the wrong discernment. It also has much the right
performance and all the wrong perception. That is the case with so much
"Christian faith" today, particularly in its numerous orthodox and "evangelical" iterations. And it is this subtle and difficult-to-discern distinction
(we can say the "little difference that makes a big difference") between
what we shall call *form and force* that thrusts into the spotlight the crisis
of Christian theology in the twenty-first century.

THE TWILIGHT OF ENLIGHTENMENT UNIVERSALISM

In January 2015 a major world event took place in Paris, France, that
reminded most people in the West of similar incidents that had rocked
America in September of 2001 and England in July 2005. I am speaking,
of course, of major "terrorist" attacks carried out by Islamic "extremists"
against the West as deliberate acts of defiance, and contempt for, what
the latter considers its peaceful, secular institutions. It is highly likely that
during the interval between the writing of these sentences and the
reading of this book that traumas of a similar, if not of an equally intense,
character may have also taken place. Every time these attacks occur, the
vast "explanation industry" (what I would call the "media-academic
complex" as a play on Dwight Eisenhower's famous "military-industrial
complex") in the West goes into high gear either to warn us that either
we have ignored the growing militant threat to our "free institutions" and
failed to take the threat of radical Islam seriously *or* to tell us why we

need to acknowledge and confess our culpability in contributing to the rise of radicalism because of our legacy of colonialism, racism, economic exploitation and so on, or we are not sufficiently sensitive to theological authenticity and dignity of Islam as a religion in itself. None of these familiar, knee-jerk responses really gets to the heart of a matter, which only a critical theology can really do. What a critical theology can do is diagnose, by a certain procedure that the philosopher Nietzsche termed "genealogical," the significance and content of the force behind the form, or the *force of God* impelling the form of faith and belief. And it can do it in a way that our now ineffective habit of looking for immanent causal schemes fails to accomplish.

The distress prompted by these Islamist attacks compels us to see the problem not so much as one of curbing "extremism," or as atonement for alleged sins of a particular people against the rest of the world's peoples, or even as encouraging what is sometimes cheaply referred to as "interfaith dialogue," but in confronting the profounder sources of the crisis. Ultimately, from a Western point of view—and that, of course, is the real starting point, as previous "genealogical" philosophers like Nietzsche or Heidegger have emphasized, for what conventionally has been known as "theology"—the crisis comes down to *a crisis of core liberal values.* The crisis arises from seemingly compatible, or negotiable, binaries within our underlying value systems, which turn out to be neither compatible nor easily negotiable. The case of Islam and its growing presence within the cultures of the West forces us to examine closely—and with a lot more tolerance for ambiguity than we would like—the significance of these binaries.

The crisis can be boiled down to one of *Enlightenment universalism,* from which so many Western juridical and political principles are derived, versus *multiculturalism.* The universalism of the Enlightenment, which spawned the French Revolution, always assumed that both human dignity and human liberty resided in fostering laws as well as institutions that would guarantee the freedom of the mind and the right to unfettered expression of the thoughts it called forth. While recognizing that what today we call "civility"—refraining from gratuitous opprobrium toward those with whom one differed, or from whom one was different—was the key to the free exchange of ideas, the paladins of the Enlightenment regarded sensitivity to cultural differences as a sign of education and breeding, not as a social or political mandate, let alone as an occasion for the intervention of the state.

This lack of concern was rooted in what now can be considered either an arrogant, or naive, assumption that a commitment to rational inquiry and discussion itself will ultimately sort out all differences, and that when one enters into the cosmopolitan concourse of enlightened conversation and respectful inquiry, one will in time realize that the importance of one's own cultural particularities is negligible in comparison to the promise of what some theorists nowadays have termed rather quixotically a "global civil society." Such a society would, in principle, be awash with blessings of what Kant envisioned as an emergent universal community of enlightened beings treating each other as "ends in themselves," a new secular universal "religion" circumscribed "within the limits of reason alone."

What later critical theorists such as Max Horkheimer and Theodor Adorno dubbed the "myth" of Enlightenment began to unravel almost from the start, especially with the Napoleonic wars. But the myth was finally busted by the New Left in the 1960s and 1970s, which itself was inspired by the work of the younger and more radical members of the Frankfurt school such as Herbert Marcuse. For Marcuse and those like him, the heritage of the so-called Age of Reason turned out to the valorization of "instrumental" reason far more than "critical" reason. Instrumental reason transformed faith in the power of reason into a faith in the mere capacity for science and technology to improve material life and "deliver the goods," effectively mobilizing and shrewdly managing the world for the sake of our private narcissistic impulses in order to maintain the hegemony of consumer capitalism.

Marcuse, who became the darling of what we now call "cultural Marxism,"[35] did not think this trend meant that Enlightenment rationalism and universalism should be abandoned, only that militants should, fueled with the adrenaline of reinvigorated Hegelian dialectics that elevated the role of "critical reason," take the Enlightenment where even the Enlightenment had never dared to go. But Marcuse's admirers, especially in America, took matters in a different direction. The shocks to the militant idealism of the time, represented in such page-turning events as the assassinations of Martin Luther King Jr. and Robert Kennedy and the election of cold warrior Richard Nixon in 1968, sent the once unified left in different directions. Many white radicals became disillusioned and rudderless, and capitulated to what they called the "system," as the movie *The Big Chill* in the seventies so dramatically and poignantly rubbed in. At the same time, minority communities discarded MLK's "I have a dream" rhetoric, full of the sentiments of both traditional Christian and Enlightenment universalism, and began to construct narratives of ethnic exceptionalism and self-exclusion from the cultural mainstream.

The new strategies of critical theorizing emphasized the underlying marginalization, noninclusion, "silenced voices" and even subtly sanctioned violence of the presumed "Eurocentrism" and "phallocentrism" invisibly propping up the "hegemony" of universalistic[36] norms and narratives. A countermyth of what technically became known as "heteronormativity" itself went mainstream, first in the academic world and gradually in Western society at large. The new normativity of "multiculturalism"—or what in today's somewhat stilted jargon has come to be termed "inclusive excellence" —took on its own subtle "hegemonic" aura. The new "categorical imperative" of recognizing and celebrating "difference" increasingly became the unchallenged metanarrative of our times.

Multiculturalism and the Narrative of Inclusive Difference

Ironically, the narrative of inclusive difference did work fairly well for a while to incorporate nonwhite Europeans into the very social and economic fabric that neo-Marxist criticism and the emergent "identity politics" had sought to unmask, as woven through with the hypocritically exclusionary standards of Enlightenment universalism. It did so well that

in 1997 Žižek stepped on a lot of "progressive" toes around the world
when he declared,

> The conclusion to be drawn is thus that the problematic of multiculturalism—
> the hybrid coexistence of diverse cultural life-worlds—which imposes itself
> today is the form of appearance of its opposite, of the massive presence of
> capitalism as universal world system: it bears witness to the unprecedented
> homogenization of the contemporary world. . . . So we are fighting our pc
> battles for the rights of ethnic minorities, of gays and lesbians, of different
> life-styles, and so on, while capitalism pursues its triumphant march—and
> today's critical theory, in the guise of "cultural studies," is doing the ultimate
> service to the unrestrained development of capitalism by actively partici-
> pating in the ideological effort to render its massive presence invisible.[37]

The same kind of dynamic continues to operate—unwittingly, according
to Žižek—for many "leftists" who have come to insert Islam in general and
even militant Islam in particular into those portfolios of those abused by
capitalism, when in fact it is the very same "kinder and gentler" capitalism
into which they in their ivory towers and hip urban bistros and micro-
breweries have bought and from which they have swallowed whole without
so much a twitch of ambiguity or unease. Writing in the New Statesman in
the immediate wake of the Paris trauma, Žižek is even more blunt. Islam
cannot be folded simply and accordion-like along with a whole variety of
ideological trinkets signifying "the Other" into the multiculturalist's hope
chest, he says. The tendency to do so on the part of Western progressives
is not a sign of their enlightenment, but their decadence. Their attitude
toward illiberal acts of violence by the same Other, summarized in the
French saying tout est pardonné (all is forgiven), which the second Charlie
Hebdo caricature of Mohammed mocked, constitutes a kind of thinking,
according to Žižek, that institutionalizes the latest iteration of Nietzsche's
"slave morality" and the pervasive attitude of ressentiment as the hallmark
of Western culture. "Such thinking," writes Žižek,

> has nothing to do with the cheap relativisation of the crime (the mantra of
> "who are we in the West, perpetrators of terrible massacres in the Third World,
> to condemn such acts"). . . . For these false Leftists, any critique of Islam is

denounced as an expression of Western Islamophobia. The result of such stance is what one can expect in such cases: the more the Western liberal Leftists probe into their guilt, the more they are accused by Muslim fundamentalists of being hypocrites who try to conceal their hatred of Islam.[38]

Pulling no punches, Žižek goes on to compare Western intellectuals and especially wannabe leftists to Nietzsche's "Last Men."

Over a century ago Nietzsche perceived how Western civilization was moving in the direction of the Last Man, an apathetic creature with no great passion or commitment. Unable to dream, tired of life, he takes no risks, seeking only comfort and security, an expression of tolerance with one another. That portrayal summarizes perhaps the pathology of today's reactive academics, the new social media intelligentsia that prefers scoring on daily points of political dyspepsia than engaging in any probing critical analysis of what is happening around them. For Žižek, the Islamists do need to be defended because their "passionate intensity" mirrors pathetically the loss of any grand vision of life, even the vision of Enlightenment universalism of which the new "tolerance" is a distant echo and *devolved* type of dysfunctionality. "It effectively may appear that the split between the permissive First World and the fundamentalist reaction to it," Žižek opines, "runs more and more along the lines of the opposition between leading a long satisfying life full of material and cultural wealth, and dedicating one's life to some transcendent Cause."[39]

At the end of the essay Žižek calls for a genuine, committed new radicalism that transcends multicultural mumbo-jumbo and embraces once more the universalistic vision of emancipation, which of course he frequently and familiarly argues can only be conceived in terms of a reborn, Marxian Fourth International. Žižek forgets that the multiculturalist position is a direct descendant of the Marxist critique of ideology and has been aimed at Western tribalism, the real implication of the term *Eurocentrism*. In many ways German chancellor Angela Merkel's recent alarmist observation that "multiculturalism has failed" throughout Europe is a recognition that the rhetoric of inclusion for ethnic minorities from the Baltic to the Mediterranean, putatively anchored in the ideal of universal human rights pertinent to the charter of the European Union, has never been able to compete successfully with the age-old tribalism of race, language and cultural memory that fostered the respective European national identities in the first place.

But what multiculturalism does *not* get at all is Islam, which has never been a form of ethnic self-designation. Rather from the seventh century onward it was always a vision of the universal transformation of the social and political order through a militant response to the unconditional will of Allah as revealed in the Qur'an. That is something Žižek discerns but to which the multiculturalists are blind. In fact, Olivier Roy has built his career on showing how the growth of militant Islamism in Europe is an indigenous and self-conscious form of resistance to multiculturalism comparable to that of European nativists, who believe that only people who share their own national racial or cultural identity should be given citizenship. The global era of a rainbow-hued cultural pluralism administered by the invisible hand of an ever-generative consumer capitalism is over. The struggle to define a genuine and perhaps ultimately successful new form of universalism that will bind the planet together is now beginning.

What would such a new universalism possibly look like? Until the 1960s, the basis of any notion of a political universalism derived from what were generally considered prima facie Enlightenment assumptions. The genesis of universalism could be located in the procedures of what Kant termed "pure reason," the kind of rigorous formalism assigned as the intrinsic method of science and mathematics that, when applied to moral or political (if not religious) affairs, yielded incontestable conclusions to which any "rational being" would have to assent. In philosophical jargon, this approach of Kant came to be known as the "principle of universalizability," which at various levels and in different contexts also was gradually assumed to be the basic rule of *verifiability* for ethics as well as all empirical inquiry. The two ideological engines of the Cold War—democratic liberalism and revolutionary Marxism—*both* adhered on their own terms to the Enlightenment stance, claiming in effect that their "bourgeois" or Communist opponents manipulate the discourse either consciously or unwittingly in order to disguise certain "particularist" preferences (capitalist control of the means of production or the dictatorship of the party elites) as universalistic rules or categories.

However, in the intellectual environment of the Vietnam era, which provoked an unprecedented attitude of iconoclasm among Western intellectuals and prompted so many of them to call into question even the most cherished secular pieties of the modern era, Enlightenment universalism came under sustained attack. Enlightenment universalism had been invoked consistently to brutalize and dominate indigenous peoples with their tribal identities and worldview, the critics charged. Moreover, scientific rationality had been discredited not simply with the devastating weapons technology of mass warfare used against much simples peoples such as the peasants of Southeast Asia, but as was evidenced in the cold, dehumanizing "Nazi science" of the World War II concentration camps. Finally, even "scientific" Marxism was not immune, as feminists and representatives of different ethnic or gender constituencies pointed out that it discounted the emancipatory potential of cultural identity as opposed to economic class. The so-called New Left of America and Europe rebelled against the old "materialist" doctrines of what was essentially Stalinist Communism and began to sketch the contours of what would later be designated as "cultural Marxism." The newest forms of critical theory provided the conceptual grist for many of these reformulations of old-school Marxism.

ENLIGHTENMENT UNIVERSALISM AND COLONIALISM

American sociologist Immanuel Wallerstein is one of the most prominent critics of Enlightenment universalism. Wallerstein cites, in particular, the oft-invoked military "right of intervention" against "barbarous" actions by non-European governments, as we have seen repeatedly in Africa, during the Balkans wars of the late 1990s, in Iraq and in Libya. Wallerstein insists that, practically speaking, Enlightenment universalism has served as subterfuge for ongoing strategies for subjugating non-Western peoples, with the aim of maintaining the reach of neoliberal market capitalism. Wallerstein's central argument focuses on his claim that there have been certain "crucial and large scale notions over time to legitimize power: the right to intervene against barbarians; the essentialist particularism of Orientalism; and scientific universalism."[40] Wallerstein would agree with Žižek that the subtext behind these notions has been to ground and legitimate the inexorable expansion of capitalism over time. In a much earlier essay from the late 1980s, Wallerstein wrote that "there are two main ways of explaining the origins of universalism as an ideology of our present system. One is to see universalism as the culmination of an older intellectual system. The other is to see it as an ideology particularly appropriate to a capitalist world-economy." In addition, these two ways of regarding universalism "do not necessarily contradict each other."[41]

One strategy, which has gathered quite a lot of interdisciplinary currency recently, can be found in the work of Walter Mignolo. In his groundbreaking work *Local Histories/Global Designs*, Mignolo drafts the elements of what he designates as "post-occidental reason." Without any elaborate or sophisticated philosophical inquiry into its origins, Mignolo identifies— as have philosophers from Kant to Heidegger to Žižek—the crisis of Occidental reason as due to its epochal failure to wiggle out of its centuries-long entrapment in the metaphysics of the subject, or *self-referentiality*. It is because of the "impossibility" of breaking out of such self-referentiality that Mignolo radically transposes Descartes's notorious *cogito ergo sum* ("I think, therefore I am") into the "I think where I am." Mignolo's point of departure is no longer "personal" or "individual," but a collective and cultural *site-based* thinking.

Mignolo's site-based approach, which he lays out in detail in *Local Histories/Global Designs*, is intimately tied up with what counts as his signature contribution to contemporary discussions on globalization: his critique of modernity. Mignolo's general thesis is that colonialism and the history of social and political dominance over non-Western people cannot be explained merely as political, economic and martial projections of Western civilization. They derive ultimately from the very worldview and ways of thinking that have characterized the West and that distinguish them radically from non-Western peoples, a difference that Mignolo, in borrowing a turn of phrase from the Peruvian sociologist Anibal Quijano, calls the "colonial difference." The colonial difference comes into play historically when modernity morphs as the official ideology of global expansion following the discoveries of Columbus. It leads to Western military and commercial subjugation of everything—and everyone—beyond the European and North American perimeters.

The "modern," henceforth, is no longer a way of thinking, but becomes a "world system" of both discourse and knowledge designed to reorganize political boundaries, modes of expression and ethnicities as well as gender markers and labor relationships. Everything is thought of as a strategy of *domination through communication*, according to Mignolo. Mignolo characterizes thought that operates within the modern/colonial and is able to think the authentic difference between modernity as such and a modernity that can be simultaneously conceived from the "other side" of the equation. Thinking not only from this side but also from the "other side"—that is, from the standpoint of people who do not think like Westerners—Mignolo dubs "border thinking." "Border thinking structures itself on a double consciousness, a double critique operating on the imaginary of the modern/colonial world system, of modernity/coloniality."[42] This "double critique" is also well in line with—and reinforces—internal critiques of modernity that have come through such "postmodern" philosophical movements as post-structuralism (popularly known as "deconstruction") and identity theory. Mignolo maintains that what distinguishes border thinking is that, even though it has no specific, established discourse of its own, marking out a position from which it operates (e.g., the "Western tradition"), it is a force, or complex assembly of forces, in its own right. It belongs to "the relocation of languages and knowledge in the current stage of globalization," which in turn give rise to "the emergence of new local actions with an international agenda." Furthermore, "these new social actors are, at once, contesting the idea that global designs can only emerge from one particular local history and resetting the rules of the game."[43]

In his latest major book *The Darker Side of Western Modernity*, Mignolo is of course less sanguine about the capacity of border thinking as

he outlined it a decade earlier to displace the colonial/modern economy
of language and power. Modernity itself remains resistant to changes in
this economy. In place of "border thinking," Mignolo sets forth what he
dubs the "decolonial option." Contrasted with the famous Cartesian "I
think, therefore, I am," decoloniality is no longer about thinking what or
where one is, but "I am where I do." Mignolo puts it quite bluntly. "A
decolonial question would be: 'Why would you like to save capitalism
and not to save human beings?' 'Why would an abstract entity be saved,
and not the ecological and human lives that capitalism is constantly de-
stroying?' . . . That is how modernity/coloniality works."[44] Mignolo distinguishes between what the philosopher Gilles Deleuze would term two
different "images of thought" that make decoloniality a strong moral
imperative when it comes to rescuing human beings from the relentless
expansion of the Cartesian imperium, in which even our favored "Continental philosophies" today are ingloriously trapped. This relentless expansion takes place, as did the ancient Roman imperium, in the name of
humanitas, according to Mignolo. *Humanitas*, as the sign of the modernist imperium, is an "epistemic zero point," an unsurpassable site of
cognitive certitude, out of which arise "'human concepts' of natural
reason," the rage to construct through the "disjunctive synthesis" of a
relentless differentiation of terms and concepts, running all the way from
Descartes through Kant, to the identity theorists themselves.

But this rage for "rational classification," the secret addiction of modernity, also "meant racial classification," that is, "who establishes criteria
of classification and who classifies."[45] The rational sovereign who decides
who is "subject" also classifies, and in this process of classification, determines who is "other" and who is "not," who is "in" and who is "out." This
kind of classification goes all the way back to the Roman Empire, when
only those who conformed to the imperial norms of "civilization" (which
was the same as subjugation) could be considered "human." In fact,
Mignolo draws his own distinction between the notion of the *modern*,
rational, Cartesian subject, which he designates by the Latin term *humanitas*, and the masses of peoples who do not live up to Enlightenment

norms (whom he describes as *anthropos*, the Greek term for what it means to be human in a minimal sense). The "decolonial" option constitutes a cry of insurrection among the cognitively dispossessed against the tyranny of the differential rationality of the Enlightenment, which generated the different religious, social and educational distinctions that have given us colonialism, racism and the vast modern administrative apparatus (what the Michel Foucault calls "biopolitics") that feeds off this classificatory system. If a critical theology is able to hear this cry, it must do something that the classical Western theological enterprise has not done, or only quite clumsily accomplished. It must address the question of the "religious" head-on and straightaway in a manner that theology is not always comfortable with, or accustomed to.

4

The Question of Religion

*True universalists are not those who preach
global tolerance of differences and all-encompassing
unity, but those who engage in a passionate struggle for
the assertion of the Truth which compels them.*

SLAVOJ ŽIŽEK

THE FRANKFURT SCHOOL AND THE PROBLEM OF RELIGION

In the most important work the early Frankfurt school and its merry band
of critical theorists produced, titled *The Dialectic of Enlightenment*, Max
Horkheimer and Theodor Adorno challenged the very notion of "objectivity" not only on scientific but also on ethical grounds. By the "ethical,"
I mean nothing more than the way such an intellectual dogma has affected the concrete and personal lives of myriad individuals in a variety
of cultural contexts. From a strategic vantage point, Horkheimer and
Adorno argued that the real outcome of the dialectic of Enlightenment is
not mutual respect for all "rational beings," as Kant had envisioned it, nor
some kind of long-haul, universal commitment to "reasoned" standards
of good conduct and social justice, but the triumph of an *amoral* and
apolitical calculus of means regardless of the aims. The authors cited the
Marquis de Sade, from whom we derive the term *sadism*, on account of
his exaltation of human perversity and the pursuit of satisfaction for even
the cruelest and most bizarre kinds of desire, as the genuine legacy of the

Enlightenment. Reason is not, in reality, the instrument of a disinterested moral universalism, the authors insisted, but

> the organ of calculation, of planning; it is neutral with regard to ends; its element is coordination. More than a century before the emergence of sport, Sade demonstrated empirically what Kant grounded transcendentally: the affinity between knowledge and planning which had set its stamp of inescapable functionality on a bourgeois existence rationalized even in its breathing spaces.[1]

From an economic standpoint, according to the authors, the true legacy of the Enlightenment is the dogma of the "free market." The market is invested with its own kind of mystique, advancing as the aggregate outcome of multiple, competing "free choices," which are supposedly "rational," but only in the sense that reason is perceived as promoting self-interest (*amor soi*, or "self-love," as the Enlightenment called it).

The obsession with free choice also implies a theoretical justification of immorality—or at minimum amorality. "The market economy [the Enlightenment] unleashed was at once the prevailing form of reason and the power which ruined reason."[2] For Kant, there is nothing more "rational" than the subjection of arbitrary inclination, or what today we would term "consumer" choice, to the mandate of reason. Kant's famous formulation of the so-called categorical imperative derives from this insight: "Act only according to that maxim through which you can at the same time will that it become a universal law."[3] In other words, reason disciplines the will—it regulates its egoistic impulses—to act for the benefit, and in consideration, of all human beings. Kant regarded this moral "universalization" of the principle of choice through "pure reason" (*reine Vernunft*) as the very founding doctrine of the Enlightenment itself.

Nevertheless, there was also another side to the Enlightenment exaltation of pure reason, and a wholly different logic can be located in the tradition of so-called British empiricism, starting with the seventeenth-century philosopher John Locke and running through the writings of nineteenth-century thinkers such as Jeremy Bentham and John Stuart Mill. These figures, otherwise known to us nowadays as "classic liberals," emphasized the inherent rationality of what on the surface seemed like "irrational," or largely capricious, decision making. Adam Smith, the father of modern economics, enshrined this seemingly counterintuitive notion in his account of an "invisible hand," which transformed the aggregate of individuals seeking their own self-interest into a social good. Later, Bentham and his followers, who came to be known as "utilitarians," urged legislators themselves to honor this seemingly paradoxical precept by seeking to advance "the greatest good for the greatest number," or what they termed a "felicific calculus" that would ensure everyone's private advantage might somehow be factored into a political equation that advanced the public good overall. It was this "libertarian" take on the meaning of the Enlightenment as "enlightened self-interest" that spawned the glorification of calculative reason, which the Frankfurt school regarded as the demon seed that eventually spawned fascism. "For those at the top, shrewd self-preservation means the fascist struggle for power, and for individuals it means adaptation to injustice at any price."[4]

As both Locke and Smith had originally noted in their "revision" of Enlightenment morality, the driving force behind this "irrational rationality," whereby the result of all particularistic strivings is a universal beneficence or general good, is the power of desire itself. The average person is quite familiar with the guarantee of the right to a "pursuit of happiness" enshrined in the Declaration of Independence, but few may realize that the very concept and wording embedded in this familiar inscription of liberal democracy comes from Locke's own notion of self-seeking as the engine of social and political life. Only professional philosophers—and usually only those specializing in early modern thought—tend to read Locke diligently these days. Political theorists acknowledge him as the architect of what might be considered the broader theory of liberal democracy as it has been operative in the West for several centuries. But only a relatively small segment of scholars connect his quite well-known defense of individual rights and liberties, not to mention so-called laissez faire economics and arguments in favor of a minimalist role for government, which were forged as a justification for the Glorious Revolution against the absolutist Stuart kings in 1689, to his views on the origin of human knowledge.

One may ironically regard Locke as the "first philosopher" of the consumer society, though it has never been phrased in quite that manner before. Whereas the Kantian version of the Enlightenment, following a set of prescriptions that can be traced all the way back to Plato's *Republic*, centered on the subjugation of private desire to a rationality of the whole, Locke's philosophy focused on the necessity of restless striving as a spur to "industry." It is not "reason" that determines the will, according to Locke, but unfilled desire, which in his *Essay Concerning Human Understanding* he termed "uneasiness."

> What is it that determines the will in regard to our actions? And that, upon second thoughts, I am apt to imagine is not, as is generally supposed, the greater good in view; but some . . . UNEASINESS a man is at present under. This is that which successively determines the will, and sets us upon those actions we perform. This uneasiness we may call, as it is, DESIRE; which is an uneasiness of the mind for want of some absent good.[5]

For Locke, there can be no "innate idea" about what is good or righteous. Each of us must "work out our own salvation with fear and trembling," and we do so through the kind of restless activity that is constantly seeking out novel goals and objects of satisfaction, which can never find a final equipoise or equilibrium, at least in this life. If Kant, the German pietist, believed that the inculcation of a universal morality (what he termed a "religion within the limits of reason alone") can lead to the implementation of a universal commonwealth, Locke, the Puritan advocate of what Leon Trotsky would later dub "permanent revolution," maintained that refractory human willfulness could be redeemed by letting it follow its own course. If Locke did not exactly swear by the assertion of the now infamous antihero of capitalism Gordon Gekko from the movie *Wall Street* that "greed is good," he at least understood the excesses of desire as it trenched on the limits of avarice as being ultimately responsible for promoting in a backhanded manner the "public good." And it is this very Lockean metaphysics—what the historian Peter Vierick has called a "metapolitics"—of both the human condition and the nature of political organization that, according to the Frankfurt school, led the Enlightenment astray.

Odysseus and the Critique of Global Consumer Capitalism

The Frankfurt school, of course, was not so much interested in a moralistic critique of personal self-seeking as in the way the dysfunctions of what could be perceived in the early 1940s, when *The Dialectic of Enlightenment* first appeared, as an emerging global society seemed increasingly irreversible. Horkheimer and Adorno interestingly found the paradigm for this new global dysfunctionality in Homer's *Odyssey*. Odysseus, the military hero turned global wanderer, succeeds not only in combat but also in his mastery of the art of survival, which he does through a "cunning intelligence" and a chameleon-like aptitude for adapting to any situation (*polytropos*). More than anything, however, he desires to return home to Ithaca, where his kingdom and his faithful wife Penelope await him.

The story of Odysseus in retrospect can be taken in itself as a trope for the experience of the millions of American GIs during and after World War II, who following the defeat of the Axis powers did everything they could to carve out their own personal islands of family bliss and social stability during the late 1940s and the entirety of the 1950s. Although the authors of the *Dialectic of Enlightenment* did not directly foresee the postwar period, their analysis anticipated the growing idolization of science and technology and its use to manage and control society during that era as the very incarnation of what they designated "instrumental reason." Consumerism itself as a strategy of personal salvation, as well as its promotion through mass advertising and the manipulation of people's anxieties, ideals and wants, as remembered today iconically through the popular AMC series *Mad Men*, became the norm. Enlightenment thus became, in the immortal words of *Dialectic of Enlightenment*, a form of "mass deception" in the form of mass entertainment, what the authors named the "culture industry." "The more strongly the culture industry entrenches itself, the more it can do as it chooses with the needs of consumers—producing, controlling, disciplining them; even withdrawing amusement altogether. . . . But the tendency is immanent in the principle of entertainment itself, as a principle of bourgeois enlightenment."[6]

Horkheimer and Adorno had in mind the social passivity, or mass hypnosis, the power of the "culture industry" could produce. It was what Guy Debord, a Marxist theorist and political radical who rose to the prominent in the 1960s with his concept of "situationism"[7] and "culture jamming "[8] (an approach that more recently was adopted successfully by the Occupy movement in its publicity assault on economic privilege and income inequality), called the "society of the spectacle."[9] Critical theory had always claimed that its ultimate mission was to foster a theoretical perspective that could be seamlessly integrated with a certain "emancipatory praxis." The focus of the Frankfurt school, in contrast with orthodox Marxism, on the character of culture rather than economic systems and structures, was intended to create conduits for human liberation at a time when previous mass movements that claimed the mantle of emancipatory theory and practice, especially Stalinist Communism, had turned totalitarian and betrayed their own promises.

The Frankfurt school discerned strong totalitarian tendencies within the very new ideology of "freedom" promulgated by the Western democracies as they confronted the international ambitions of the Soviet Union. The "freedom" of market-based democracy masked the enslavement of the mind itself by the entertainment industry as it both stimulated and regulated the spheres of human desire and social awareness. "Critical theory" struggled to counter "enlightenment as mass deception" by new programs and pedagogies that occupied themselves with advancing what we presently refer to as "critical thinking." But there was one dimension of culture that the critical theorists scrupulously—and strangely—ignored. That was religion. Unlike Marx, the Frankfurt school neither attacked organized religion, which in the postwar period became something of a national obsession, nor sought to revision it, as many of their academic heirs starting in the sixties did, as something emancipatory in its own right. Marx himself had proclaimed in the opening sentence of his *Critique of Hegel's Philosophy of Right* that "the critique of religion is the prerequisite of every critique."[10] But for the Frankfurt school, it was not religion, but *culture*. The Frankfurt school tacitly rephrased Marx's dictum. The critique of culture is the premise of all criticism.

However, as we ascertain these days, culture cannot be divorced by any meaningful account from the reality of religion. In fact, so many of the contemporary heirs of critical theory, who rely in some respect on the critical perspective that Marxist social analysis has provided from time to time, have not only come to realize that religion itself has its own *critical* application but have also discovered that religion, rather than serving as the object of critique, is its very *subject*.

BADIOU AND ŽIŽEK—VANGUARDS OF A NEW CRITICAL THEORY OF RELIGION

The two current thinkers I have selected, as mentioned earlier, to illustrate how religion becomes the subject of the new critique—and henceforth the linchpin of the new critical theory—are Badiou and Žižek. We begin with Žižek. In *The Puppet and the Dwarf*, a book that appeared right after the turn of the millennium, Žižek offered his rather complex and ambivalent take on the Christian faith, which he has ironically sought, like Marx and Engels before him, to identify as a kind of precursor to Communism.

> My claim here is not merely that I am a materialist through and through, and that the subversive kernel of Christianity is accessible also to a materialist approach; my thesis is much stronger: this kernel is accessible *only* to a materialist approach—and vice versa: to become a true dialectical materialist, one should go through the Christian experience.[11]

Žižek's long-standing interest in Christian thought first became evident in *The Ticklish Subject*, where Žižek charts a course for his theory of subjectivity. The following year *The Fragile Absolute*[12] came into print and was followed by *On Belief*,[13] which engaged with certain questions that were left dangling throughout his earlier writings. Several years later Žižek, in *The Monstrosity of Christ*,[14] also sparred directly in an interlocutory bout with John Milbank, a prominent theologian and leading light of the movement known as radical orthodoxy. Žižek's aim has never been to conflate Christian doctrine with theories of materialism itself or construe it simply as an antiquated kind of political philosophy. On the contrary, Žižek argues in effect that the historical problems with which the early Christians were confronted, and that still occupy us nowadays, cannot be decisively addressed either by familiar Christian claims of a divine agency acting from outside what philosopher Charles Taylor terms "the immanent frame" or through popular materialist forms of explanation. Christian transcendentalism and Marxist historical materialism desperately need one another, and can mutually and fruitfully provide critical leverage for each other, Žižek suggests.

For Žižek, Christianity and historical materialism function as accountability partners in a regime of so-called tough love. This antagonistic correlation of the interests of each party toward the other results in the "splitting" of what Žižek refers to as the "subjective position" of each of the parties. Žižek draws such an argument, as well as these sorts of analogies, from his distinctive combination of the views of the French psychoanalyst Jacques Lacan and the philosopher Hegel, the "gray eminence" of critical theory. Throughout his career Žižek has offered several different idiosyncratic readings of Hegel through the lens of Lacan. He expands on the Lacanian insight, cobbled together over time with patients struggling to come to terms with what it means to articulate oneself as a subject (i.e., to speak of an "I"), that the act of affirming a position— especially an ideological position—invariably involves a rupture between one's immediate sense of "subjecthood" and the desired aim of such an affirmation. This discord is experienced as a split in the subject itself, which Lacan represents as the "barred S" ($), resembling a dollar sign. Or, in more technically psychoanalytical terms, the subject is split, or sundered, because it consists in the ongoing "signifying relation" (S/s in the notational symbolism of structural linguistics) between the conscious and the unconscious, between what we are fond of saying and what we actually mean without saying it.

In his book titled *The Parallax View*, which he once characterized as his magnum opus, Žižek explores through various examples and analogies—

both cultural and scientific—the implications of this disjunctive signifying relationship as an "impossible short circuit" where things juxtaposed with each other appear to make sense, even though any kind of conceptual "synthesis" is out of the question. The notion of "parallax," which he takes from physics and otherwise refers to the seeming displacement of objects arising from different points of observation, therefore replaces both the crucial principle of "negation" in both the Hegelian and Marxist dialectic and the concept of "ontological difference" that we find in later twentieth-century philosophy, particularly Martin Heidegger. In his more recent books such as *Absolute Recoil: Towards A New Foundation of Dialectical Materialism* and *Less Than Nothing: Hegel and the Shadow of Dialectical Materialism* Žižek locates such a "short circuit" in Hegelian philosophy itself, on which Marxism of course is based. What Hegel describes in the final paragraphs of his massive tome *The Phenomenology of Spirit* as the "Golgotha of Absolute Spirit," or the death of God on the cross, becomes the "zero point" not only for the full disclosure of the meaning of Christianity itself, but also for the recognition of the Lacanian split subject as the key to *ontology* as a whole, and hence as far more than a useful psychological metaphor. Žižek writes in *Absolute Recoil*,

> The final reversal [in Hegel's *Phenomenology of Spirit*] is crucial: the disparity between subject and substance is simultaneously the disparity of substance with itself. This reversal takes place at all levels: subjectivity emerges when substance cannot achieve full identity with itself, when substance is in itself "barred," traversed by an immanent impossibility or antagonism; the subject's epistemological ignorance, its failure to fully grasp the opposed substantial content, simultaneously indicates a limitation, failure, or lack in the substantial content itself; the believer's experience of abandonment by God is simultaneously a gap that separates God from the believer, an indication of the "unfinished" nature of the divine identity, and so on.[15]

In other words, it is God's "unfinished" nature expressed through the revelation of substance as a kind of "failed" subjectivity (the passion of the Christ) that becomes the secret of the movement of history, including a materialist history as well as a historical materialism. At the same time,

Žižek does not see Christian theology as any kind of "answer" to what is at bottom an issue for philosophical materialism. Christianity exposes the chink in the armor of classical forms of materialism and provokes its radical reinvention, as the subtitles of his two works insinuate.

At the same time, Žižek's role as a "fellow traveler" with historical Christianity and with the Christian theological tradition can be viewed in the same light as "postmodern Marxists" such as Terry Eagleton and Badiou himself, who have also found inspiration in the legacy of Jesus' followers. Badiou is exceptionally important in this regard because of the reception of his book *St Paul: The Foundation of the Universalism*, published the same year as *The Puppet and the Dwarf*. The release of the former treatise caused quite a stir because of Badiou's renown as an unrepentant Maoist and atheist. Yet, as Badiou himself explained,

> For me, truth be told, Paul is not an apostle or a saint. I care nothing for the Good News he declares, or the cult dedicated to him. But he is a subjective figure of primary importance. . . . For me, Paul is a poet-thinker of the event, as well as one who practices and states the invariable traits of what can be called the militant figure. He brings forth the entirely human connection, whose destiny fascinates me, between the general idea of a rupture, an overturning, and that of a thought-practice that is this rupture's subjective materiality.[16]

Badiou—and in certain measure Žižek—has discerned in Paul's connection with Jesus Lenin's relationship to Marx. Without Paul Christianity would have remained an obscure cult of Palestinian Jews devoted to a crucified would-be messiah. Without Lenin Marxism would have persisted perhaps as a kind of arcane intellectual rendering of the more militant strategies of Europe's growing labor movement in the dawning era of social democracy. "I am not the first," Badiou writes, "to risk the comparison that makes of [Paul] a Lenin for whom Christ will have been the equivocal Marx."[17] Yet Badiou is also uncompromising about his attitude toward the religious side of Christianity. "Let us be perfectly clear," he insists, "so far as we are concerned, what we are dealing with here is precisely a fable."[18]

Badiou expends much of his effort in *St. Paul* showing how Paul's view of Jesus' resurrection as the fulcrum of faith has little to do with the apparition of a restored physical body, as the Gospels report. The resurrection, according to Badiou, means little in the concrete context in which the disciples claimed to have witnessed it. However, in the hands of Paul, this "unprecedented gesture consists in subtracting truth from the communitarian grasp."[19] Paul's proclamation that the resurrection has happened is "subtracted" from the historical contingency of what might have actually taken place outside Jerusalem in the fourth century AD, depositing a *form* of universality that becomes "the ruin of every attempt to assign the discourse of truth to a preconstituted historical aggregate."[20] From Badiou's standpoint the meaning of resurrection is not *whether* it actually occurred. The resurrection belongs to the process of signification Badiou elsewhere dubs a "truth procedure." The importance of the resurrection is that it mobilizes *as truth* an act of fidelity to a promise of universal redemption. In that respect it is, as Badiou indicates, the "foundation of universalism" generated from a singular moment marked by an unprecedented experience on the part an obscure little band of Galileans that will ultimately count as the "messianic" fulfillment not only of previous Jewish narratives but also as the truth for all peoples for all time. It is such "fidelity" to a universal, motivating truth that Badiou regards as the dynamics of political revolution down through the ages.

As far as Badiou is concerned, Paul is the "militant" of truth. Truth is "entirely subjective," according to Badiou. But that does not relativize truth. Truth can only exist in the situation of a militant activist who struggles every day to maintain fidelity to the universal truth governing his or her commitments and calls forth unswerving allegiance. The "fidelity" of a militant "to the declaration [i.e., the declaration that Christ is risen] is crucial, for truth is a process, and not an illumination." In addition, "a truth is of itself indifferent to the state of the situation."[21] Instead, truth is measured by the power of the collective act of fidelity. The gestation of this movement of truth in response to a universal injunction can be called the "truth-event."

It is in this regard that we can begin to understand Badiou's distinctive rendering of what he thinks Paul means by "faith," the faith in the risen Jewish Messiah that "justifies" us once and for all in the sight of God.

"The apostle is neither a material witness, nor a memory," Badiou claims. It is not incidental that Paul did not know Jesus in the flesh. Paul's "declaration" can in no way factor in discrete memories of who Jesus was, or what he did, or the "historical" fact of the resurrection, which as we saw Badiou terms a fable.

> [The resurrection] is not, in Paul's own eyes, of the order of fact, falsifiable or demonstrable. It is pure event, opening of an epoch, transformation of the relations between the possible and the impossible. For the interest of Christ's resurrection does not lie in itself, as it would in the case of a particular, or miraculous, fact. Its genuine meaning is that it testifies to the possible victory over death, a death that Paul envisages . . . not in terms of facticity, but in terms of subjective disposition.[22]

To be preoccupied with the long-vanished eyewitness testimonies or material circumstances in which a forensics or retrospective "science" of the resurrection might be put in place in order to settle the question of whether it ever really did "happen" is sheer pretense and folly. The truth event is not something that can be calculated as to its veracity for a neutral observer. To the contrary, "The event is measurable only in accordance with the universal multiplicity whose possibility it prescribes. It is in this sense that it is grace, and not history."[23]

It is such an observation that distinguishes Badiou, as it does a figure such as Žižek, from the kind of "dogmatic" materialism routinely associated with Marxist dialectics, or the kind of "vulgar" materialism much in vogue nowadays in the West. Badiou's rather nuanced approach aligns him straightforwardly with the tradition of critical theory first introduced by the Frankfurt school. Especially in its later phases, the Frankfurt school was highly "critical" of all garden-variety materialisms, which it associated with late consumerist capitalism.

BADIOU AND THE EVENT

The Frankfurt school recognized that certain "idealist" strains of thought could harbor tremendous emancipatory potential, inasmuch as they served not just as powerful "transcendental" critiques of the established order but also as motivating and *mobilizing* sparks for revolutionary un-dertakings. For Badiou, the "event" is both the occasion and the promise for an unprecedented transformation of the world as we know it. According to Badiou, the event is much broader in scope than the singular "split" that happens at a certain moment when the affirmation of the subject and the insurrectionist act takes place. The ultimate "evental" site, henceforth, is Golgotha itself, when "God renounces his transcendent separation." Such a renunciation is what Badiou terms an instance of "grace," which changes the direction of the course of history. As a result, God "creates, not the event," but "its site." The evental site becomes the nucleus of the composition of the event itself, "addressing it to *this* sin-gular situation, rather than another."[24] The death of Christ serves as the "site" for Badiou's truth event, which is the experience of the resurrection and its impact on others from that time forward. The resurrection as event is the engine of historical action and transformation. The event "redistributes" the trajectories of historical meaning and the will to action. The event itself is only made possible by the "splitting" of the historical subject at the site of its occurrence—in this case marked off for all time perhaps by the disjunction between the expectation of Jesus' followers concerning his mission and destiny as Messiah, the "savior of Israel," and the humiliation of the cross followed by his wholly unanticipated ap-pearance on Easter morning to the women and later to the disciples. The "grace" implicit in this unforeseen series of circumstances is what recon-figures the significance of history as *Heilsgeschichte* (as the German theo-logians would call it), that is, "salvation history."

What makes Badiou's take on the universal significance of Rudolf Bult-mann's "Christ event" is that it shifts the language of critical theory from what Hegel and Marx regarded as the "power of the negative"—or the thrust of dialectical rationality—to what Christians understand as "faith." Faith, for Badiou, therefore functions as the term that "names" the sub-jectivity of the subject in the composition of the truth event. What Badiou in 1 Corinthians regards as Paul's "third" discourse, the discourse of "Christ crucified" (1 Cor 1:17-25), wielded in opposition to the Jews who "seek signs" and the Greek philosophers who demand cogent arguments, is the enunciation of a universal instance of "becoming-subject" marking fidelity to the event. And, as Paul suggests in the opening chapter of his initial letter to the Corinthians, there can be no extrinsic "demonstration" of the truth of this event. The truthfulness of the truth event resides in the new discourse of collective fidelity, the "faith" of the witnessing community. "It is not the singularity of the subject that validates what the subject says; it is what he says that founds the singularity of the subject."[25]

For Badiou, the Christ event "testifies to the possible victory over death, a death that Paul envisages . . . not in terms of facticity, but in terms of subjective disposition." It is Badiou's contention that the Pauline—like the Lacanian—subject *arises in the moment of division*. "For, in reality, one subject is the weaving together of two subjective paths, which Paul names the flesh (*sarx*) and the spirit (*pneuma*)."[26] Such a distinction corresponds to the difference between life and death, because "it is of the essence of the Christian subject to be divided, though fidelity to the Christ event, into two paths that affect every subject in thought."[27] Badiou interprets the Pauline opposition between death and life as a *mode of subjectivity*. The subject signifies an intermingling of the two dynamic processes. The *subject becomes subject by avowing the truth of the event*. It is this avowal, according to Badiou, that accounts for what Paul really means by the familiar theological expression *sole fide*, or "justification" by "faith alone."

Paul's familiar diatribes against the Pharisaic interpretation of the Torah, or "law," can now be better grasped. The law leads to "death" insofar as it is "considered in its particularity, that of the works it prescribes, the law blocks the subjectivation of grace's universal address as pure conviction, or faith."[28] Highlighting the particularity of the divine regulation, the law is inherently incapable of expressing any form of universal content. The law is forever subordinated to its own contingencies, qualifications and partialities. In contrast, however, grace is "that which occurs without being couched in any predicate, that which is translegal, that which happens to everyone without an assignable reason. Grace is the opposite of law insofar as it is what comes *without being due*." In consequence, according to

Badiou, *"that which founds a subject cannot be what is due to it."*[29] In fact, Badiou (in what he with obvious paradox refers to as a "materialism of grace") argues that the word commonly translated in the Greek New Testament as "faith" points to this founding act of *subjectivation*.

> Resurrection summons the subject to identify himself, as such, according to the name of [*pistis*]. This means: independently of the results, or prescribed forms, that will be called works [according to the law]. In the guise of the event, the subject *is* subjectivation. The word *pistis* (faith, or conviction) designates precisely this point: the absence of any gap between subject and subjectivation. In this absence of a gap, which constantly activates the subject in the service of truth, forbidding him from rest, the One-truth [the universalist truth of indifference to difference via militant fidelity to the event of truth] proceeds in the direction of all.[30]

For Žižek, however, Badiou's reading of the Christ event is way too simplistic. Drawing on the Freudian background of Lacan's thought and not merely the formal elements of philosophy (which he criticizes Badiou for doing), Žižek insists that the question of the law is really one of a "perversion," inasmuch as it is the law itself that prompts the very transgressions of the law, a problem on which Paul expounds at length in his epistle to the Romans. Žižek asks, "How can I break out of this vicious cycle of the Law and desire, of the Prohibition and its transgression, within which I can assert my living passions only in the guise of their opposite, as a morbid death drive?"[31] Badiou, of course, employs as his touchstone the "event" (*l'événement*) of truth as that which marks subjectivity in the zone of life rather than death.

But for Žižek one cannot easily dismiss the power of Freud's "death drive" manifested in the paradoxical fact that zealous adherence to the law ensues not in eternal life, but in sin and death. According to Žižek, it is "tempting to risk a Badiouan-Pauline reading of the end of psychoanalysis, determining it as a new Beginning, a symbolic 'rebirth'—the radical restructuring of the analysand's subjectivity in such a way that the vicious cycle of the superego is suspended, left behind." However, that would be a misuse of Lacan, for whom psychoanalysis resists all syntheses within the

realm of subjectivity. And especially for Lacan, "Negativity functions as
the condition of (im)possibility of the enthusiastic identification—that is
to say, it lays the ground, opens up space for it, but is simultaneously ob-
fuscated by it and undermines it."[32] Psychoanalysis shifts the equation away
from life in the direction of death. In Žižek's words, "Lacan parts company
with St. Paul and Badiou: God not only is but always-already was dead—
that is to say, after Freud, one cannot directly have faith in a Truth-Event;
every such Event ultimately remains a semblance obfuscating a preceding
Void whose Freudian name is *death drive*."[33]

The major difference between Badiou and Žižek is that, in the case of
the latter, the subject cannot be assimilated even by a tortured logic to the
process of *subjectivation*. Žižek's uncompromising refusal to permit any
kind of reconciliation, whether philosophical or theological, follows his
own rigorous adherence to the Lacanian model. Anterior to all gestures
toward subjectivization, according to Žižek, the subject cannot be distinguished from the utter negativity of the death drive in its naked reality.
"Lacan's point is not that the subject is inscribed into the very ontological
structure of the universe as its constitutive void, but that the '*subject designates the contingency of an Act that sustains the very ontological order of
being.*'"[34] In effect, Žižek resists any effort to avow the universality of the
truth event as embraced by the subject in the account given us by Badiou.
Instead, "the subject is the contingent emergence/act that sustains the
very universal order of being."[35] Furthermore, Žižek's approach does not
allow for what Christian thinkers, or would-be "materialist" thinkers such
as Badiou, would identify as "faith." But, strangely, Žižek—even though
he is committed to the finality of the idea of the "death drive," as featured
in both classical and Lacan's own "revisionist" form of psychoanalysis—
does open up certain recognizable theological horizons in his implicit
development of what we might regard as a notion of grace.

ŽIŽEK ON THE CRITICAL CHARACTER OF CHRISTIANITY

The gist of Žižek's approach can be found in his 2001 book *The Fragile Absolute, Or Why Is the Christian Legacy Worth Fighting For?* In the book, as

the subtitle implies, Žižek inquires whether Europe as the "proper" site for the historical preservation, historical development and worldwide diffusion of Christianity can be saved in a meaningful way. He also raises the question whether the Christian legacy will ultimately be preserved in the future as a secular transform through which the economies of the world are reengineered in accordance with the dictates of global capital or whether the spirit of the risen preacher from Galilee can be a force for egalitarianism and revolutionary praxis. As far as Žižek is concerned, that is the fateful pass at which Europe as a civilization has arrived. It was a question that, at the time, was on the minds of much of the European intelligentsia, particularly in view of the lofty promises held out by the leaders of the fledgling European Union. Although the EU was technically a "secular" project, it served often to invoke in the memories of its proponents the once glorious age of "Christendom," a theme that the papacy of John Paul II and his lieutenant Cardinal Ratzinger made no bones about fomenting.

Žižek raises the possibility that the failed hopes of secular Marxists might somehow be requited by having a new look at Christianity while pondering the plight of the animal world. He cites the German philosopher Friedrich von Schelling's observations concerning the "infinite melancholy of all living nature." It is, he says, "as if living nature itself was secretly pointing towards, waiting and longing for, the emergence of *logos* as its redemption." Žižek connects Schelling's metaphysical image of nature in need of redemption to Fellini's attempt to make a film "about a universe in which Christianity is yet to come, from which the notion of Christian redemption is totally absent."[36] It is this kind of grim world, which may indeed be the world we inhabit, from which we need to posit a sort of "Christianless" (my term) Christianity in which salvation does not take place on any kind of otherworldly, or *extraworldly*, plane of meaning, but can be understood in terms of the very dialectics of desire and rage that the psychoanalysis historically has focused on.

Žižek rethinks the conventional view that eternity is "beyond" time, or is some kind of timeless space that constantly intersects with the here and now. On the contrary, eternity signifies a traumatic event that opens

up time in "the first place." Eternity as trauma constitutes "the point of
'eternity' around which time circulates."[37] What makes Christianity distinctive, according to Žižek, is that it rejects the instinctive religious tendency to renounce the experience of time, which is also the realm of
discontent, anguish and suffering, in order to attain the ecstasy of eternity.
As a counter to the world-denying tendencies of so many of the world's
great religions, what Christianity "offers [is] Christ as a mortal-temporal
individual, and insists that belief in the *temporal* Event of Incarnation is
the only path to *eternal* truth and salvation."[38]

But Žižek wants to go further and provide a "deep" psychoanalytical
reading of the Christ event itself, something Freud infamously attempted
in *Moses and Monotheism* as well as *Totem and Taboo*. The psychoanalytical perspective merely reinforces the strange kind of cosmology
that Schelling in the nineteenth century advanced, mainly that the Fall
is not some primordial disaster due to human willfulness and disobe-
dience, but both follows from the nature of God and occurs eternally
within the divine nature itself. Hence, the Christian equation of the
execution of the Messiah on the cross with the "death of God's own son"
correlates directly with the myth of a primordial murder, which Freudian
psychoanalysis sought to uncover as the key to the neurotic condition of
civilization itself. Christianity is distinctive because it acknowledges that
salvation is founded on trauma. Or, in Žižek's words, it is "ready to
confess the primordial crime (in the displaced form of murdering not the
Father but Christ, the son of God), and thereby *betray* its traumatic
impact/weight, pretending that it is possible to come to terms with it."[39]

This primal trauma of Christianity itself is reminiscent of Schelling's own
"cosmological" explanation of the persistence of a suffering world. In his
earlier work Žižek oscillates constantly in his use of comparisons to the point
he is driving home between psychoanalysis and Schelling's metaphysical
accounts of what went on prior to the history of the world. Žižek writes,

> Schelling's problem is not "what does God mean in our—human—eyes?" . . .
> Schelling's starting point is always God, the Absolute itself; consequently, his
> problem is: "What role does the emergence of man play in the Divine life?

Why—in order to resolve what kind of deadlock—did God have to create man?" . . . It is only in man, in human history, that God fully realizes Himself, that He becomes an actual living God.[40]

Man is "similar" to God because God, in Žižek's interpretation of Schelling, has his own timeless "neurotic" conflicts. Christianity "confesses" in its own founding story such a neurosis and redeems history through its very en-actment. Unlike Judaism, Christianity in its preoccupation with prohibi-tions against the free play of desire, wrought by the force of a God-ordained Torah, shatters the cycle of law, desire and transgression—and the attendant divine wrath—and resolves the problem by "killing" God over and over, an insight that Nietzsche perhaps sought to communicate in his famous parable of the madman. Christianity fulfills Lacan's imperative of coming to terms with one's own impossible desires. "Enjoy your symptoms" is Žižek's celebrated reformulation of how one in good psychoanalytic fashion overcomes the insanity of wanting what is prohibited *because* it is prohibited. Christianity, therefore, no longer has any reason to avoid confronting *the deadlock that is internal to God*, the traumatic incommensurability between the life of the Father and the life of the Son. What psychoanalytic theory terms "split" subjectivity is a dysfunction lodged within the eternal nature of God, and the incarnation does not "take it up and cancel it" (Hegel's a dialectical synthesis), but lays it bare for us all to savor and revel in.

Žižek codes this "downward synthesis" of the Hegelian resolution, or *Aufhebung*, in terms of Schelling's speculations. It offers us a hint of what Žižek might really have in mind with his idea of a "grace" that is at the same time "materialist." Žižek asks, "What if God's descent to man, far from being an act of grace toward humanity, is the only way for God to gain full actu-ality, and to liberate Himself from the suffocating constraints of eternity? What if God actualizes Himself only through human recognition?"[41] Grace in Žižek's sense is not given to humanity by God. Instead, it must be con-strued as an "event," the event of incarnation. The moment of God becoming human is simply what grace signifies. God's sublation (the ascent) is a downward synthesis (the descent) into material embodiment: grace is what happens when God becomes human. It consists in "the non-coincidence of

man with man, the properly *inhuman* excess which disturbs its self-identity
. . . the monstrous surplus" that signifies the irreducible *identity* of God and
(hu)man. Christ *is* Adam, and "the problem with the Fall is thus not that it
is in itself a Fall, but, precisely, that, *in itself, it is already a Salvation which
we misrecognize as a Fall*."42 The story of the fall is indistinguishable from
"salvation history." "It is not that the Fall is followed by Redemption: the Fall
is *identical* to Redemption. . . . The explosion of freedom, the breaking out
of the natural enchainment—*and this, precisely, is what happens in the
Fall*."43 In contrast with Badiou it becomes clear that grace, according to
Žižek, does not designate the *event of truth*, which is the resurrection. Grace
is the *truth of the event*, and the event in this instance is the duplex movement
of fall *as* redemption that is interior to God's own "timeless" self-expression.
Christ is what Žižek terms the "monstrosity" amounting to the *excess* of the
human within the dynamism of the divine itself.

If Schelling provides the towering metaphysical framework through
which Žižek works out his own curious version of a "materialist" theology,
it is the Gospels themselves that point toward a politics that is both
"Christian" and world transformative in the way Marxists have always envisioned. True to his "materialist" orientation, Žižek takes the core
Christian principle of *agape* and renames it "political love." Moreover, such
a political love reenacts collectively within world history the "redemptive"
process that comes down to God *materializing* as the excess of the human
over the divine. With his own *psychoanalytical* take on Paul's theology of
incarnation that differs decisively from Badiou's theory of the event, Žižek
understands *agape* as a kind of "insurrectionary" force that challenges the
prohibitions of the law, the mechanism for both the repression and functional redirection of desire that capitalism orchestrates. However, this challenge does not take place from "outside" the circuit of law and transgression.
In an entirely paradoxical manner the power of "political love" remains
within the cycle, yet at the same time it breaks the circuit insofar as the new
"freedom" and the "new creation" that marks the status of the subject who
is now "in Christ" has been released from the obsessive and compulsive
demand of the Freudian superego to obey the "law."

As a historical sidelight, we might note that biblical theologians, often because of their Reformation heritage, are accustomed to mystifying Paul's concept of the law as something unmistakably Jewish, Pharisaic and thus *religious*, whereas the word (*nomos*) that Paul applies throughout his writings is the same term that Hellenistic speakers used for all social rules and political obligations. In consequence, the strong, secular implications of *nomos* offer some evidence for the kind of thesis Žižek advances about salvation as a mode of liberty from what Lacan establishes as the inexorable "law of the father," inscribing a psychological as well as a theological alternative to the dialectic of desire and transgression, as well as to the divine wrath and existential annihilation ("the wages of sin") that, so far as the circuit itself is drawn, logically follow. What Christianity, with all its "monstrous" moral ramifications, prevents is the urge to transgress the law, inasmuch as it is the impulse itself that completes the cycle.

The issue is not that the subject is torn between the law and sin. The subject itself is incapable of telling law from sin. As Paul himself writes in Romans 7, "Once I was alive apart from the law; but when the commandment came, sin sprang to life and I died. I found that the very commandment that was intended to bring life actually brought death" (Rom 7:9-10 NIV). If sin is not an exception to the law, but enfolded within the law itself, the Christian is not technically "emancipated" from the law. As orthodox theological commentators have argued for two millennia, in opposition to libertines and gnostics, Paul's theology of "freedom in Christ" does not entail *antinomianism*, a systematic violation of or—at best—an indifference to the restraints of the law. Contrarily, the Christian as *subject* is no longer *subjected* to the law as law, but to the law *within* the spirit of love. Žižek explains the "political" meaning of this kind of subjection in *The Monstrosity of Christ* when he replies to Milbank's question: "If law as such . . . is also crime, then wherein lies the good for Žižek?" In answer, Žižek proclaims that the good "is not in the domain of law, which is by definition caught in a self-propelling vicious cycle with crime, but in love—not in sentimental love, but in love on account of which, as Kierkegaard put it with his matchless radicality, I am ready

to kill my neighbor."[44] Here Žižek extends the meaning of *agape* to include what is unabashedly political. Christianity is the prototype of what
Žižek, employing militant Marxist nomenclature, refers to as the "fighting
collective." While the logic of capitalism favors individual choice and the
satisfaction of desires in consumer goods and the abstract signs of consumerist fantasies (Marx's "fetishism of commodities"), Christianity sub-
ordinates private inclinations to a completely different sort of imperative,
the imperative to respond to God's *eschatological* call for the restoration
of the creation as a whole.

CHRISTIAN MILITANCY

Theologically speaking, we can say that the political order as we know it is
part of "fallen" creation. But the Christian militant of "faith" belongs to the
creation that is the very primal expression of God's essence, as the incarnation has signified all along. In other words, the "monstrous" excess of
humanity within the divine comes to be manifested in history as something akin to what Derrida has labeled a "new internationale" whose
"specter" continues to "haunt" the present system, even the system we know
as global capitalism.

Žižek roundly attacks the various types of "New Age" spiritualities that
have proliferated in the West since the 1960s. New Age religious pluralism
is merely the flip side of consumer capitalism, and like multiculturalism
it serves as a powerful instrument of ideological control over people's
desires. Žižek opts instead for "the emancipatory potential in institutionalized Christianity," by which he does not "mean state religion, but . . . the
moment of St. Paul."[45] Like New Age pluralism, which is thinly disguised
latter day paganism, "the idea of the Gospel, or good news, was a totally
different logic of emancipation, of justice, of freedom."[46] For pagans, "injustice means a disturbance of the natural order." However, the gospel
message consists in a "radical abandonment" of the idea of a natural
balance that must be restored, even by state violence when called for. The
gospel starts from the "zero point" of an unprecedented freedom in Christ,
which amounts to "radical equality" that makes absolute, eschatological

demands on us all. This "messianic" anticipation belongs to a "totally different world whose formal structure is that of radical revolution. . . . The past can be erased; we can start from the zero point and establish radical justice, so this logic is basically the logic of emancipation."[47]

But this kind of faith does not require "belief" in a transcendent order, or any assent to some kind of providential scheme of history whereby the risks we take in defying the status quo ante are calculated as somehow worthy of our sacrifices. We do not take the radical plunge required of all militants, including the "church militant" consisting of apostles, missionaries, martyrs or even heretics, because we must act (in Kant's well-known postulate in his *Critique of Practical Reason*) "as if" there were some final guarantee that we will be rewarded and that cosmic justice will prevail. Faith, by Žižek's reckoning, is nonetheless a radical new "Christian" subjectivity, a stance of the truth-militant that recognizes that there can be no emancipation with any warrant or objective guarantees at the end. The gesture of faith is a "groundless" one, which *activates*, and actuates, salvation with a "cold cruel passion." It is what Žižek terms the "political suspension" of the ethical, which is another name for *agape*.[48]

In both Badiou and Žižek, we encounter a radical reading of Christianity and its "soteriology," or conception of "salvation." Neither Badiou nor Žižek is interested in personal "spiritual" struggles that are relevant only for specific individuals. They are concerned about the larger collective, historical and *political* significance of such a soteriology. In that respect, neither figure even comes close to addressing the traditional as well as familiarly *doctrinal* questions theologians have asked for centuries. Nor would it be proper to say that they are engaged in some kind of "edgy" discourse regarding social ethics, which often derives from more conventional theological warrants. What both of them succeed in doing is not only to *rewrite* the very agenda of the theological enterprise itself from a "political" point of view but also to provoke and probe profoundly into the *extratheological* context in which theological language itself has not hitherto seen itself situated. It is this repositioning of theological language that begins to define what exactly we mean by a "critical theology."

Traditional critiques of theology usually end up proposing certain *non-theological* procedures and protocols that might do a better job than the way of going about things that theologians themselves are wont to do. But a critical theology, like critical theory, does not trifle with methodological substitutions, or seek to water down the aims of theological thinking through "reductionistic" accounts of what theology actually is supposed to be. A critical theology gets to the heart of the motives of theology at its very center and depths as a "critical enterprise," not as a "handmaiden" to philosophy or any field, nor as an instrument of ecclesiastical outreach, nor even as the true "understanding," as the Augustinians would have it, of what faith achieves when it becomes intelligent and self-conscious. Like critical theory, a critical theology is *emancipatory* in the measure that it frees us from all the ideological conceits and theoretical modes of *over-determining* the human condition that so many secular and influential nontheological "theories" routinely make. But in order to get a better perspective on how that emancipation might be conceived, we need to look at the theoretical question of the "religious" itself.

5

Toward a Theology of the "Religious"

*If you don't know the difference between theology
and religious studies, then you're a theologian.*

BRIAN BOCKING

THE EMERGENCE OF "RELIGIOUS
STUDIES" AS AN ACADEMIC FIELD

While "theological" pursuits in the last half century have often focused
on explicitly Christian, quasi-Christian, crypto-Christian, New Age or
"perennialist" themes that still bear the mark of a Western viewpoint, the
so-called *study of religion*—or "religious studies"—has refused to engage,
almost to an obsessive degree, in both the theoretical and theological
tasks by focusing, sometimes exclusively, on selective anthropological
and historical particularities that satisfy the unstated secularist criteria
for what still remains a "Eurocentric" method of inquiry. A global critical
theology, however, would seek to facilitate the deconstruction of the
ever-seductive Western "myth of objectivity" as well as the false "insider/
outsider" dichotomy in which present-day scholarship has trapped itself.

One of the main reasons the Frankfurt school downplayed—or even
ignored in some cases—religion, according to scholars Margarete
Kohlenbach and Raymond Geuss, was its unswerving allegiance to the
standards of empirical rigor, as was common among Western academics
through most of the twentieth century. "It is difficult, but perhaps not in
principle impossible," they write, "consistently to combine an empirical

modification of the Marxist critique of religion with a view that ascribes emancipatory potentials to religious practice and thought."[1] The notion that there might be an "empirical" rather than a theological approach to the question of religion would have struck the typical scholar of that period as odd, to say the least. With the growth in prestige of the social sciences during this same period, however, things began to change at a quickening pace. The growth of the field of anthropology, which relied heavily on the data of beliefs and practices of native peoples colonized by the increasingly secular Western powers, allowed for an abundant harvest of data regarding the connections between religious belief and practices and "primitive" as well as "traditional" modes of social organization. Since the 1960s "empirical" investigations of religion have become gradually institutionalized in the youthful field of "religious studies." Much is known now from a putatively "disinterested" or scholarly point of view about the way in which religion as a whole, and specific religious identities and modes of practice, function in complex historical, cultural, social and even political contexts. But the expansion in empirical understanding of what is misleadingly named the "phenomenon" of religion has come in many ways at the expense of the deeper *meaning* of religion and its import for the "critical" dimension of theory and knowledge that the Frankfurt school prized, and that it ascertained—perhaps overoptimistically—in the power of "reason" as German idealism, more so than the *philosophes* of the Age of Reason, had conceived it.

The lack of the critical function—or what this author himself a while back branded the "default of critical intelligence"[2]—in religious studies has not been without long-term consequences. A consensus is growing that the study of religion, as an academic field, is bearing its greatest challenges since its emergence in the late 1960s. The rise of religious studies as a discipline in the previous generation was propelled largely by theologians and philosophers who sought to traverse the boundaries between "confessional" or "sectarian" approaches to the subject, the supposedly "neutral" field of comparative religions and classical anthropology. In a nutshell, the birth of the field can be described as a timely merger of interests among mid-twentieth-century liberal theologians who recognized that Christian confessionalism was no longer viable within the secular academy, the students of Mircea Eliade, the leading progenitor of the contemporary discipline of "comparative religions," and the admirers of the famous anthropologist Clifford Geertz, whose exploration of native religious practices with a keen theoretical eye and startling literary panache won him an extensive following across an interdisciplinary range of researchers. At the same time, the growth of a pop, post-Christian spirituality among the baby boomers—later incarnated as the curious contemporary syncretism we know as the New Age movement—fueled student interest in the emergent field of study. From its inception, religious studies was a conglomerate of different intellectual agendas responding to a historically contingent set of market conditions.

A commitment to an "empirical" method of studying religion, shorn of any theological presuppositions, has served as a truly politically correct stance in the last half-century, especially when cultural and religious pluralism has become the established norm, not only within higher education but also within our civic culture overall. Cultural pluralism has also implied methodological diversity. Religious studies scholars have been wont, as University of Chicago scholar Wendy Doniger once quipped, to "*poly*-methodoodle all the day."[3] "Polymethodology" is by no means unheard of, or even unusual, within the social sciences and humanities. Academic psychology, for example, runs the gamut from the "hard science" of neuropsychiatry to the pastoral and quasireligious forms of clinical and counseling therapies. Even philosophy spans the interminable, and seemingly unbridgeable, divide between Anglo-American empiricism and Continental phenomenology. But the latitudinarianism native to well-established modes of inquiry such as psychology, sociology or literary criticism differs from the fragmentation of perspectives and purposes that afflicts religious studies. There is a much wider gulf between the "myth studies" of a Jungian analyst and the ethnography of a "South Asian religions" specialist than, say, between a cultural anthropologist and an archaeologist. A loose thread of coherence binds the various strategies of "empirical" inquiry into the realm that constitutes "anthropological" subject matter. The existence of these affiliate structures of investigation is tacitly acknowledged by the suffix -ology, as in the word anthropology.

It is significant that such a suffix has never been added to the word "religion," though the phrase religiology is both orthographically and stylistically convenient. The fact that this phrase was never coined, or at least attained an acceptable level of use, during the infancy of the field, is more remarkable than it has appeared at first blush. There were at the time, of course, and still are, "departments of religion," but this nomenclature betrayed what kinds of academic enterprise such rough beasts were indeed—departments that taught religion from the standpoint of a certain broad faith commitment, if not advocacy. The convention among the field's practitioners of converting the word religion to its adjectival counterpart and inserting the inchoate expression studies also suggests, almost by way of Freudian indiscretion, what the aim was from the beginning.

The founding of the field of religious studies was, in actuality, even if not so recognized by its adherents, an attempt to pluralize the dominantly Christian—and by and large Protestant Christian—confessional community by introducing competing types of "sectarianism" masquerading as the study of what the historian of Robert Ellwood called "alternative altars," or non-Western traditions.[4] From the beginning, religious studies was a strategy of "deregulating" and opening up to global competition the praxis of theological espousal. Religious studies never aimed to be a "science" in the sense that even the "human sciences" could be regarded as such, that is, as a focused and unified means of finding commonality amid heterogeneity. Religious studies was in itself a semiconscious, deconstructive move against Protestant thinking, all the while remaining bound to the Protestant, pietistic and antihegemonic norms of its Protestant predecessors. In short, what religious studies, in contrast to most humanities "disciplines," excluding so-called area studies, has decidedly lacked is theory.

The shyness of religious studies researchers toward elaborating broad, theoretical discourses that might somehow explicate what religion is all about can be accounted for in part as the consequence of the passing in the last generation of what was known as "philosophical theology." The animus toward "theological" statements by the positivist social sciences has also been a critical factor. But the frequent pretense of religious scholars that they are offering some kind of "objective description" of the beliefs and praxes they have entertained is routinely belied by their refusal to generalize beyond the swatch of cultural materials in question. In other fields, even the narrowest trajectories of historicist investigation have drawn on operative theories.

Finally, it could be argued that the refusal to generalize ensues simply from the tendency within a youthful discipline to play it safe politically, and that religious scholars are a notoriously timid lot. However, even this straightforward observation misses the mark, inasmuch as the field in its early phases had a rich reserve of "theoretical" resources, which were neither Christian nor theological, on which to bank. The movement toward an "anthropology" of religions, which overtook the field in the late 1960s and early 1970s and was inspired by Geertz's writings, never really gained currency. Nor has the fashion of "cultural and critical studies" in the humanities, as a whole, made much headway to date among religious specialists, which still consists largely of historians, ethnographers and linguists.

One problem in recent years has been the almost total eclipse of the philosophy of religion within the study of religion, even though philosophy itself has witnessed what Hent de Vries refers to as a "turn to religion" since the late 1990s.[5] While the new post-structuralist philosophies spilling out of France provided a wealth of opportunities for assessing religion in its cultural matrix, those kinds of presentations have been decidedly absent in the examination of religious issues. Even though religion is almost by definition what Jürgen Habermas would term a system of "communicative action," no effort has been made to deploy the exploding genre of communication theory in the analysis of religious phenomena.

Theory is contentious in the academic environment nowadays because it offers unsettling questions about what religious people actually think and do, and how these modalities of signifying praxis compete and challenge each other. As both Marxists and the sociologists of knowledge have discovered along the way, the passion of religious belief can be an upsetting and destabilizing element. Whether we are talking about the millennial visions of the Diggers during the Puritan Revolution of the seventeenth century or the Islam-configured tribalism of Chechnyan fighters in the present Russia, the capacity of religious fervor to unravel the pragmatic governing arrangements of the political privileged is substantial. Theory therefore poses embarrassing considerations of how religious ideologies might in certain instances cast a violent, or disturbing, shadow over the peaceful *imperium* of global civilization seemingly unified under the banner of stock trading and currency arbitrage.

The major shortfall in the theoretical analysis of culture in general, and religious culture in particular, has been the loss of a credible strategy of critique with the death of grand narratives. The collapse of Marxism worldwide, as both a form of revolutionary consciousness and a type of post-Christian theodicy, has been more significant than many "theoreticians" care to admit. So much of the burden of theory in the last twenty years has been carried by so-called cultural Marxists, who take their cue not only from Jean-François Lyotard but also from Fredric Jameson. It was Jameson who recognized that the key to postmodernity, and postmodernism as a movement in philosophy, the arts, literary criticism and theological inquiry, lay in what Perry Anderson has called the "dedifferentiation of cultural spheres."[6] In the modern period, and with respect to modernism itself as a kind of broad, conceptual picture of the strands of that epoch's culture, the trend was always toward totalization and the varieties of explicit as well as covert fascism—the incorporation of cultural forms by the state, the immanentization of religious life and the spiritualization of both the materiality of labor and the law of exchange. Culture is concealed within the general forms of political theory and historical reflection. Ironically, the sudden implosion of Marxism signaled the liberation of the "cultural principle" from its former prison house of ideology. Whereas Marxism as a modernist strategy of interpretation had always circumscribed its understanding of culture within the dialectics of capital, postmodernism as a type of "post-Marxism" not only delineated cultural theory as separate from political economy also but made it overarching and central.

Religious Theory as "Semiotics"

As most observers have pointed out in recent scholarship regarding the odyssey of postmodern thinking, the catalyst for the reconceptualization of Marxism was Jean Baudrillard. While the transition among European Marxist theorists during the 1960s and 1970s, from the "negative dialectics" of Jean-Paul Sartre to the full-blown cultural materialism of a Louis Althusser or the long-deceased Antonio Gramsci, is a complicated story of the failure to comprehend contemporary history adequately, it was Baudrillard who first grasped clearly that the force of capital had mysteriously morphed into the power of the sign. Similarly, for Baudrillard, what Marx had termed the "relations of production" had now been transformed into the semiotics of desire and consumption. Even as the so-called consumer capitalism of the postwar era had been exhaustively analyzed by economists, the changeover from nineteenth-century modes of social and political reflection had barely penetrated the "humanistic" disciplines.[7] Baudrillard saw, and identified in terms that were far less tendentious and jargonistic than Jameson could have mustered, the symmetry between late capitalism and the explosion of the communications industry. The "cultural logic of late capitalism," as Jameson called it, is not a logic at all. It is a process whereby the rationality of cultural expressions and subdivisions gives place to what Baudrillard terms the "excrescence" of images and representations in an expanding orgy of signification.

At one level, of course, it is possible to read Baudrillard merely as a philosopher who discovered a language to account for commercial advertising, the cult of media celebrities and the Dionysian character of pop culture. But Baudrillard's insights are not to be trivialized. In the post-Marxist age, the practice of theory per se is on the verge of achieving a new currency through the comprehension of all that is "cultural" in its myriad and diverse guises. The explanation is not all that opaque. The "dedifferentiation" of the realm of culture itself means the terrain that was heretofore a kind of "plantation" for certain specific ecologies of intellectual inquiry has now become common ground for all the disciplines. That dedifferentiation has had an especially strong impact on the study of religion. Were it not for methodological "warlordism"—narrow and inherently self-legitimating foci of scholarship—that dominates the field today, religious studies would be frolicking in the sunlit fields of cultural analysis. Paul Tillich's insight that religion is the "form" of culture is more pertinent at the turn of the millennium than it was in the early postwar era.

The flowering of what is gradually coming to be known as "postmodern faith"—the syncretic, experiential, individualistic and media-dominated modalities of spirituality that have assumed the somewhat misleading labels of "New Age" religion or "postdenominational" Christianity[8]—fulfills Baudrillard's dicta. Postmodern religion is a vast, and dedifferentiated, circuit of cultural signs and metaphors that do not add up to anything resembling what religious studies scholars in the past have identified as "movements" or "traditions." Postmodern religion is the motivational undercarriage of postmodern culture as a whole. Whether we are talking about metaphysical seekers who chant to the "ascended masters" using quartz crystals,[9] or urban Pentecostals who discover "gold dust" on themselves after having received "miraculous healings,"[10] or Christian rock singers who can hardly be distinguished in their demeanor or music from other pop musicians, we are no longer entering into some arcane, academic discourse about "dialogue" among Buddhists, Hindus, Jews and Christians. We are no longer even talking about "religion" as conventionally construed.

The discourse of religion under postmodern conditions adds up to what Richard Murphy terms a "counterdiscourse" that constitutes a whole new theoretical strategy.[11] Such a counterdiscourse is no longer about the "disciplinary object" we know as religion. It is not "about" anything at all, in fact, but amounts to a second order of simulation—the retextualizing, or developing, of an interpretive code for the play of performances and iconic showings that make up "religious culture." If, as Baudrillard stresses, a simulacrum is distinguishable from an entity by the fact that its "reality" can be discerned in its replication, then religious studies amounts *to a simulation of the simulacra* that precess autonomically and "chaotically" within the circulatory system of signs that is culture. The study of religion has no "subject matter"—only a sweeping and unmarked topography over which the theoretical eye may wander.

Scholars realize that the way they frame their questions and make their inferences in "doing what they do" is not some arbitrary choice or some happenstance of personal history whereby they choose to become a "sociologist of religion" as opposed to, say, an intellectual historian. The pervasive problem with the study of religion as a field is that it has resolutely and consistently engaged in the "grand refusal"—a refusal to be even minimally theoretical. The many kinds of slants have all conveyed a sense of strategically explaining religious matters mainly for academic curiosity-seekers. But in the same stroke they have proved unable to do what the study of religion with its inherent "ethnographical" proclivities could have done from the outset. They have failed to make manifest the integral and conceptual relationships among the windings and trailways of anthropological findings to such a degree that religious phenomena can be "understood" at a global level rather than simply browsed from a privileged, political vantage point.

If theory, as the classical meaning of the word intends, signifies the gaze of the theatergoer, the critical viewing eye toward a "performance," then every "theoretical" statement concerning religion must amount to something far more compelling and discerning than a mere abstract proposition about the "sacred," the "numinous" or the "spiritual." In the same way that quantum physics revolutionized our notions about scientific "objectivity" almost a century ago by positing the "observer-dependent" character of theory, so a theory of religion can overhaul our now historically obsolete habits of taking religion either as something private and confessional, or as a phantasmal castle of what the famous nineteenth-century sociologist Émile Durkheim termed "social facts." Both models are, in truth, empty idealizations. Theory is the signifying probe or "position" (in Derrida's ironical sense) that distributes the events of signifying praxis that make up the "phenomenal" order of things. Religion does not, or cannot, stand alone; it is inextricably semiotic in its texture and weave. It is "theory dependent."

A justification, interestingly, for the study of religion as what we might call a "higher semiotics" can be found in the critical method pioneered by the classical form of religious theory that went by the name of *theology*. The idea that theological thinking can be partitioned off as indications of specific "religious traditions" makes no more sense than the view that biology can be divided methodologically according to the different species under scrutiny. "Theology," stripped of its ecclesial, doctrinal or even ethnological trappings, simply betokens the "science of the divine," and that in a broad sense is what religious theory must strive toward. If one examines the different "religions," one finds that each "tradition" in its own right is "theology laden." Though the origins of both science and mathematics are shrouded within their own cultural conditionedness, their theoretical means and aims have been unflaggingly independent of the cultural formations within which they were incubated.

Theoretical thinking within the sphere of inquiry we call "religion," therefore, of necessity must be also a "semiotic" way of thinking, that is, a manner of *thinking in signs*. What do we mean by "thinking in signs"? Semiotic investigation is an essential venture into thinking through the veil of "representation." What do we mean by "representation"? Despite the tendency to contort and mystify the word in postmodern philosophy and theology, the concept of representation is not all that obtuse. As Jack Goody notes in his examination of the "representational" languages of religion, theater and art, the concept *au fond* merely implies the broader strategy of mimesis.[12] Mimetic patterning has nothing to do with replication, or copying, as Plato thought. The "mimetic" is not at any level a reduplication of the "real." Instead, it is a "redrawing," which in fact brings about a disfigurement at the site of depiction. It is an act of "reference" that in fact overcomes the referent. The "presentation" of the real invariably establishes a synecdochal style of sign-connectivity between the representation of the real and the real that is represented.[13]

The study of religion is semiotic at its core, because it is not about "words" and "things" as philosophy and logic conveniently regard them. The study of religion is about the way in which the logical constraints of the process of representation are removed yet remain "significant" at the same time. As Gary Genosko observes in his overview of the new cycle of scholarship in both semiotics and cultural studies, the pursuit of the humanities at large is a wandering in the "theater of representation." And "all representation is theological, a matter of filling gaps."[14] When one begins to frame the "theory" of religion as a theory of semiosis, or how the mimetics of representation function at an extreme level, then one can do philosophy of religion, if not "philosophical theology," in a whole new manner—as *religious theory*. Religion itself is a latticework of sign-functions and signifying elements that transcend the grammatics of common sense. These signifying elements do not coalesce into some kind of metaphysical object, as Durkheim and others have always believed. The mysterious yet theoretically inconsequential construct of "the sacred" belies this means of misconstruing the subject regions to which we append the label of religion.

The "sacred" is not an entity, nor does it consist in some kind of affective or "extrasensory" overlay to ordinary experience. The sacred implies a movement, or even a mutation, of signs whereby the mimetic relationship between the different signifying constituents is entirely asymmetrical. It is this unique asymmetry of religious semiosis, wherein the "object" signified is neither visible nor recognizable in terms of the signifier, that produces the mythical, or the numinous. The performative character of religious action accentuates this movement. When Mircea Eliade, the éminence grise of religious studies as a field, talked of religious ritual as a reenactment of sacral events that took place *in illo tempore*, he was speaking in a metaphysical vein of the asymmetry of religious mimesis's original insight that representation is an erasure, not a repetition, of presence can be located within this scheme of reference. If origin can never be recovered after the act of signification, then the *semiosis* that distinguishes religious language is such a complete rupture within the "deconstruction" of the sign that only the discourse of *wholly otherness* is possible. Religious theory is an extension of cultural theory in the measure that it opens up the hinterland of all those representations and signs that can be counted as part of human "anthropology." To reduce the study of religion to a descriptive anthropology, as has happened largely in the past several decades, is not only intellectual cowardice but also methodological malpractice.

It was initially Aristotle, and ultimately Plotinus, who understood that any account or "explication" of phenomena resides in the articulation of the relationship between terms, not as a predicative relationship, but in the ambivalent sense of what Aristotle called *prōto ti*, as an aesthetic configuration that evades every logic of equivalence. Plotinus used an expression that Stephen Gersh argues is the anchor of semiotic procedure itself—*logos tēs scheseōs*, a "rationality of relation [of difference]."[15] This rationality of the relationship between what is otherwise perceived as a "disfigured" form of mimesis, as a drawing of strange maps and impossible terrains, is the "theological" charter of religious theory. It is a rationality that is ultimately "heterological" in the sense that the early post-structuralist Georges Bataille meant it. But it is a rationality nonetheless. Semiology requires the incongruity of "the other." So-called scientific anthropology, on which the study of religion has slavishly modeled itself, has surpassed itself in this generation by recognizing that *to heteron* is not a datum of science, only an affectation. It only becomes "scientific" when it becomes heterological.

IS A "CRITICAL THEOLOGY" OF THE RELIGIOUS POSSIBLE?

We have a good idea these days about what a refurbished theory of religion might look like, or even how critical theory might be applied to the study of religion.[16] Yet, at the same time, we need to ask how these various ventures might somehow add up to the framework for a new "critical theology." Is it possible to envisage a "theology of the religious" that would be congruent, if not entirely compliant, with *both* the theological enterprise as we have come to think of it from a wide angle of vision *and* critical theory, as it was originally imagined? To tender such a phrase as "theology of the religious" without sounding redundant, we have to break decisively with the way in which "religion" has come to be construed by confessional, or evangelical, theologians, as a sort of sophisticated interior monologue that is completely divorced from the existential response of faith, or at worst must be regarded as a self-deluding habit of idolatry.[17] Likewise, we must also resist what has become the prevailing viewpoint among the Western intelligentsia that, if we are to take religion seriously at all, we must keep it at a safe distance and observe it dispassionately as one "objective" phenomenon among many others. Ironically, both extremes— even Karl Barth's well-known jaundiced account of religion as a kind of ignorant, "unformed" faith likely to lapse into the kinds of cognitive distortions and moral perversities that the apostle Paul describes in Romans 2—derives from this idea that religion is something *apparent*, namely, that it belongs to the realm of representation, that it is distinctly a "phenomenon."

A "phenomenon," as the Greek etymology of the word implies, is "what appears." In the philosophical discipline known as "phenomenology," which its founder Edmund Husserl in the early twentieth century defined as the "strictest of sciences," there is always an attempt to discover somehow the "essence" hidden behind the phenomenon. The search for the "essence" of what we call religion—a pursuit now generally dismissed by critics as "essentialism"—occupied scholars for much of the late nineteenth and the first two-thirds of the twentieth centuries. Essentialism, in the scholarly investigation of religion, has now been connected by such scholars as Tomoko Masuzawa to strategies of colonial administration and domination.[18] One can neutralize the motivational power of the phenomenon by making it something easily understandable and thus theoretical manipulable. Only when one has "tamed" religious impulses and idiosyncratic expressions of fervor by defining them in terms of normative canons along with unacceptable deviations can they be politically controlled, something the Romans discovered two millennia ago. The very notion of "world religions" or "religious traditions"—

a taxonomy accepted uncritically by virtually every citadel of higher learning—belongs to this proto-colonialist strategy of typologization.

For Foucault this strategy amounts to a *biopolitics of belief.* Foucault coined the term *biopolitics* to characterize the way in which political power in liberal democracies, including class power, is maintained through the institutions of knowledge itself and the regulation through norms of discourse and mental health of the mind itself.[19] But the sort of biopolitics Masuzawa describes has less the aim of regulating spiritual health for the sake of domestic tranquility and the seamless exercise of the "soft power" of the state apparatus. It has more to do with preventing in the name of such regulative hegemony the actual socially effective—and sometimes even insurrectionary—force that is present in religious conviction and motivation itself. It is only by reclaiming the signifying potential of religiosity per se that it can be emancipated from what Max Weber would have called the "iron cage" of the regulatory, secular apparatus of biopolitical control.

In order to achieve that goal one needs a whole new way of theorizing what is meant by "religion"—an antiessentialism that is not merely the carping kind of protests against operative theoretical meaning structures by numerous aggrieved partisans of certain presumed identities that have been excluded by the so-called dominant discourse. The dominant discourse ironically these days is *essentially* this kind of caviling identity politics of meaning. The kind of antiessentialism (or let's call it an *antiphenomenalism*) we have in mind relies on the tools and theoretical "technics" of contemporary poststructuralism—or what is popularly termed *postmodernism*—itself. It is a technics that heavily relies on the relationship between three terms that have dominated in this very powerful and prestigious discourse (a discourse tragically that has been either ignored, hijacked or lamely co-opted by the real "dominant discourse" in religious studies). These terms were first enunciated by Jacques Derrida in the 1960s, and have to this day not been appreciated for their relevance or theoretical clout. They are *sign, singularity* and *event.*

The concept of the sign comes from post-structuralism, a movement that was first launched around the time of the First World War by the French linguist Ferdinand de Saussure. For de Saussure, meaning is about the relationship between signs, which are linguistic as well as social conventions and therefore totally arbitrary. But they constitute the process by which meaning itself is differentiated. The sign is always, according to de Saussure, a *dyad* or a kind of semiotic "duplicity" out of which the *sense* of something is generated. The act of meaning is split in two between what de Saussure called the "signifier" and the "signified," or as it is written notationally, S/s. The S/s does not "refer" to a particular object, but constitutes a difference through which the illusion of reference comes into play. "Objectivity" does not correlate with a preexisting world "out there," as Kant first discovered in the eighteenth century, but with a constant and consistent structure of meaning that this process of linguistic differentiation yields in every culture. The instance of meaning, or signification, thus is not a "mirroring" of the natural order, and even if there were such an order, we could not know it apart from language. It comes down to what the post-structuralists termed the "chain of signifiers" and the differentials between each link in the chain that is made up of sequences and often complex enumerations of each S/s.

Post-structuralism was always about *force,* a notion we can trace all the way back to de Saussure's *Course in General Linguistics* and that depends not on the philosophical idea of the "concept" or the "construct" (the staple terminology of essentialism), but on the analysis of the relationship between *signifier and signified*, the key distinction in all semiotics. The force is what "moves" and drives the chain of signification. Post-Freudian psychoanalysis, especially the French school established by the important mid-twentieth-century figure Jacques Lacan, identified this force with the "unconscious" itself. The Lacanian thesis that language is driven by something we cannot name until it appears in language and its differential processes is not only one of the central insights of "postmodern" (the more popular equivalent of "post-structural") thinking in general but also figures heavily in what we are calling the "new critical theory," which links back to this tradition.

And there is a third important term that anchors post-structuralism
to this approach we call "semiotics." That is the *event*. The "moment of
difference," as "deconstructionism" would have it, is always generative of
new, dynamic sign-complexes and signifying capabilities for those iterations of language that strike us as meaningful and familiar. What "causes"
these new types of *ontogenesis* to arise and multiply, especially when we
think in terms of concrete history—Muhammad's "revelation" in the case
and the sudden eruption of warrior armies that take over the Middle
East, the crucifixion of a Galilean Jewish nobody under Roman rule in
Judea that within three centuries leads to the overthrow of the empire
itself? It is the "event," or what I technically term the "singularity," in accordance with the word used in astrophysics to describe black holes.
Black holes are singular sources of creative energy, cosmic disruption
and material transformation that do not abide by any prior rule of generative logic. They are old stars that have collapsed into themselves, but
out of that collapse emerges a new galactic "power source."

Žižek rereads the standard doctrines of materialism in this new radical
way, by claiming that what we term *dialectical materialism* has nothing
to do with a grim machinery of lifeless and soulless matter chugging
away according to the invariant laws of nature Newton first dreamed up,
but everything (on the contrary) to do with what he terms *ontological
collapse*. Something can only "be" once the idealistic machinery of explanation that we term *scientific language* breaks down. Inside a black
hole it is said the "laws of nature" themselves no longer have significance.
We must treat religious reality in this manner, and we also need to refrain
from using the term *religion* per se, thus avoiding the temptation to essentialism. Our preference should be for the phrasing *the religious*. The
"force" behind religion is a real force, and in many ways cannot be tamed
as easily as we in our managerial-rationalist fantasies, using essentialist
or quasiessentialist canons of inference, have assumed we can do.

The "religious" itself, aside from the singular events that give it origin
and sustain it, constitutes every shifting assemblages of signs and seemingly arbitrary sign-operations, which can be deployed for a variety of

seemingly unusual aims and objectives, such as *jihad* without the constraints of "just war," or "Bible churches" where no one really reads the
Bible carefully, if at all, or the multiple varieties of "yoga" that still retain
residues of the ancient ritual language while making it merely a type of
exotic calisthenics for busy urban professionals. As for philosophers eschewing the subject of religion, the problem at one level of course goes
all the way back to the ancient Athens-versus-Jerusalem dilemma. But
the challenge is even more subtle. We are at the kind of "crisis of European philosophy" that Edmund Husserl named in the 1930s, on which
the Frankfurt school picked up in its own unique fashion, and that
Heidegger in his distinctive style sought to draw attention to. It amounts
to what might be termed the *crisis of origins*. Post-structuralism has
made us aware of a crisis of conceptualization, or what this author
himself has dubbed the "crisis of representation."[20] The crisis is the same
as what Nietzsche referred to as the "nihilism" that lurks in the cracks
that were ever deepening in the proud tower of European rationality. But
the crisis of origins calls for an altogether different response from what
we are used to, not the sort of smug irony and discursive detachment
conventionally associated with popular postmodernism. It calls for a
descent into the abyss from which meanings emanate and crystallize.

THE QUESTION OF RELIGION AS AN "EXISTENTIAL" ONE

The question of the "religious" is as much an *existential question* for philosophers as it is for scholars of religion. It is the pre-Socratic Greek philosopher Heraclitus's question (which was of course Heidegger's overarching question): What do we mean by *logos*? Questions of theory,
questions of theology *and* questions of philosophy all come down to this
question. Heidegger called it the question of "originary thinking," but the
Heideggerian nomenclature, while seductive as a sort of mantra for the
post-structuralist reorientation of the mind in order to ask the question
properly, doesn't ultimately work. Our thoughts truly have to be "abysmal,"
as Nietzsche called them. A "critical theology" of the religious aims toward
a "third way" from the choice of the *via negativa* ("the way of the negative"),

or "apophaticism," and the *via eminentiae* ("the way of eminence"), that famous medieval binary. Perhaps we should designate it as the *via in abyssum* ("the way into the abyss"), a search for the molten center of the "earth" on the way to which we come across both marvels and monstrosities—as the old sci-fi movies would have us believe. Žižek, for one, has made us aware that the real and the monstrous are virtually inseparable from each other, and that goes for the "reality" of the religious.

The discourse of religion, in all its interdisciplinary instantiations, is that broad zone of minimal intelligibility that runs up against the fearful boundary that in the science of black holes is called the "event horizon," the boundary beyond which the source of what we know is catastrophically generated but remains impenetrable to our theoretical gaze. Here we have the opacity of the "event" itself from which the universe of signs, like star fields, nebulae and particles of dark matter, are constantly generated. There is no "essence" to the singularity. It is what we can name, appropriating a metaphor from the Austrian poet Rainier Maria Rilke, the "fearful angel." This singularity of the religious around which the signs of both "theology" and "belief" circulate beckons us toward a profound "critical" understanding of where the reality of faith derives from.

This reality, which cannot be assimilated to a simple subject or predicate, belongs within the ambit of "force." In semiotic theory what drives every circulation of signs is a certain force field.[21] It is what we must refer to as the *force of God*, or perhaps the force we name as such. This force manifests in key events, world-turning and world-shaping events (à la Badiou) that have no peer or historical repeatability, let alone any equivalency. For Badiou, in particular, this force manifested most singularly on the morning of Christ's resurrection. A critical theology of the religious, therefore, would grasp the workings of this force in cutting through and rendering topsy-turvy the barely visible socioeconomic structures of domination that are kept in place through the biopolitical processes, as Foucault suggests, that offer us "state security" at the expense of freedom of thought, conscience, action and speech, that mesmerize us with captive fantasies of well-being in an age when chaos everywhere rages. Only a critical theology that draws on this insight into the "abysmal" meaning of the religious, one that recognizes and theorizes the "force of God" that manifests at the threshold of the eventful historical singularity, can deal with what we are facing today. As we shall see in the final chapter, these concepts of force and event converge both temporally and "theoretically" in what Bultmann himself referred to as the "Christ event," the linchpin of any critical theology. But our effort to decipher that event eludes the usual confessional standpoint that serves as the staple zone of orientation for so much of Christian theology. A critical theology is not both uniquely "Christ-ian" and *hyper-Christian* (in the sense the signifiers of what it really implies can never be contained within any sort of framed discourse). But before I clarify where we are heading with this thought, we must first contend with the (false) distinction that tends to dominate discussions of both the theological and religious—the concept of the "secular" and the relatively recent neologism, the *post-secular.*

What Faith Really Means in a Time of Global Crisis

*No man is such a legalist
as the good Secularist.*

G. K. CHESTERON

ARE WE NOW POST-SECULAR?

According to Craig Calhoun, Mark Juergensmeyer and Jonathan Van-Antwerpen in their introduction to the book *Rethinking Secularism*, the terms *secular, secularism, secularization* and *secularity* are a "cluster of related of terms" that all have a "common linguistic root," with each one operating "in different conceptual frameworks with distinct histories."[1] The word *secular* and the word *religion* have a reciprocal relation, twin or conjugate concepts that determine each other in their core meanings. From an etymological standpoint, the term *saeculum* was not first juxtaposed with the idea of the religious, but rather with *aeterinitas*, or "eternity." The word *secular* springs from the same root as the French word *siècle*, translated "century" or "age." Over time, *secular* came to refer "to the affairs of a worldly existence and was used in the Middle Ages specifically to distinguish members of the clergy, who were attached to religious orders, from those who served worldly, local parishes (and who were therefore secular)."[2]

More recently, the "secular" has come to denote modernity, as opposed to the classical or medieval era. Therefore, as José Casanova contends, it is best to posit a broad threefold analytical distinction, distinguishing between *secularity* as an epistemic category from *secularization* as a social-historical process of institutional differentiation, and *secularism* as a political and usually antireligious ideology. According to Casanova, "the secular is precisely the basic anthropological substratum that remains when one gets rid of religion."[3] It "refers more broadly to a whole range of modern secular world-views and ideologies," which can develop into "philosophies of history and normative-ideological state projects."[4] Finally, the idea of *secularization* raises the question of *the rise or decline of religion* (as encapsulated in the question of whether humankind, America, Europe and so forth growing more religious or not).[5]

Casanova breaks down the notion of secularization into "disparate and not necessarily interrelated components": the decline of religious belief, the privatization of religious practice and the differentiation between religious and nonreligious institutions. For Casanova, such a notion also involves a theory of the "progressive decline of religious beliefs and practices," in tandem with the process of modernization, as well as "the theory of privatization of religion as a precondition of modern secular and democratic politics."[6] It is the privatization of religious belief in particular that occupies Casanova. Despite secularization, religions are no longer content to remain in the private sphere and have gone unabashedly public, often in an aggressive manner. As Casanova argues in *Public Religions in the Modern World*, religion has "deprivatized" since the late Vietnam era, a shift first noticeable with the Iranian Revolution of 1978–1979, then with the "charismatic renewal" among Catholics and Protestants and the emergence of the Religious Right about the same time, then with the collapse of Communism, and finally with the rise of Russian Orthodox nationalism, as we first saw during the civil wars in the Balkans in the 1990s and of late in Russia itself.

According to Casanova, secularization as a movement is founded on a theory of institutional differentiation between the religious and secular aspects of life and is "the paradigmatic and defining characteristic of modernity," an uncontested historical and sociological fact within contemporary discourse, insofar as it pertains to Western history. The global spread of democratic aspirations and the commitment to universal human rights continues to promote this institutional differentiation, fomenting so-called multiple modernities, or models of how each discrete society reacts to what Mark Lilla, as we saw in chapter three, has dubbed the "Great Separation" between the secular and the religious.

Furthermore, secularization as a theory of the ongoing decline of religious beliefs and practices has lately come into serious question, insofar as Europe and America are both fully developed modern societies. How does one account for this discrepancy? Will the rest of the world, which is rapidly modernizing, begin to look primarily like America or like Europe? Many claim that the data arguably suggests that the world is modernizing more in line with America, as both fully modern and largely religious. Thus the character of the current trajectories of the worldwide cultural momentum we know as "globalization" casts serious doubt on the once fashionable hypothesis that modernization and the necessary decline of religion go hand in hand with each other. As the German sociologist Ulrich Beck has put it, "Secularization theory is based on two assumptions: first, that modernization as it emerged in the European context (Max Weber called it 'occidental rationality' a century ago) is a universal process which leads to similar developments all over the world; and, second, secularization is inseparable from modernization and is as irresistible." Both assumptions have been challenged and jettisoned. Modernization does not necessarily imply religious decline. While secularity is not a necessary consequence of modernization, Ulrich Beck insists that "pluralism is."[7] Pluralization is the paradigm that emerges in the discourse of the *post-secular.*

The post-secular is, unsurprisingly, a contested concept. The earliest use of the term begins with the Catholic priest Andrew Greeley in 1966, with his article "After Secularity: The Neo-Gemeinschaft Society: A Post-Christian Postscript." For Greeley, the post-secular referred to the Neo-Gemeinschaft Catholic communities that were forming within the larger organized church, and were characterized as "small, subparochial, or transparochial fellowships of believers which will give new depth and meaning to the collegial and functional Church resulting from the Vatican Council."[8] When one reads the literature of the post-secular, one obtains "a general intuition that classical theories of secularization are insufficient to grasp the present state between religions and contemporary societies and/or political arrangements," and alternatively, "a stance that there is a need, from a normative point of view, to find more just ways of accommodating religious claims in liberal institutions."[9]

SOME CHARACTERIZATIONS OF THE POST-SECULAR

The post-secular can be delineated as a critique of the classic secularization thesis, where modernization equals secularization. Greeley recognizes that modernization no longer necessarily implies secularization as an iron law. Religious revival can follow modernization. Greeley also notes how the theoretical and historical constructions of the concepts "religion" and "secular" closely intertwine with each other. The secular is an imagined space just as religion is, both as Western constructs. Secularism is recognized as ideology. In addition, multiple secularizations follow multiple modernities. For Greeley, the "post-secular" is characterized by "optionality." Secular beliefs, along with religious beliefs, are relativized as one option among many. Finally, he affirms the trend of religious pluralism and pluralization in the public square, and opens a space for coexistence, mutual adjustment and overlapping consensus between secular cohorts and religious communities. Religion has a legitimate place. That, in a nutshell, is what we mean by the now frequently used, and often overused, word *post-secular*.

The post-secular is an age where both the secular and religion are flourishing, rising, declining, developing and transforming all at the same time. The post-secular can be descriptive, when used to signify the resilience of religion in contemporary society. A post-secular society is heterogeneous, but not necessarily an enclave society. There is mutual recognition of the reality and legitimacy of "otherness" within the shared public ambience. As Vincent Geoghegan writes, "A post-secular perspective therefore betokens not a rejection of the secular, but a recognition that the achievements of the secular will not be lost by a more nuanced approach to religion."[10] One helpful way, according to Geoghegan, to interpret the post-secular in its historical context is to compare it to the era of the postmodern.

> The development of postmodern discourse is instructive for making sense of the post-secular, insofar as postmodernism can be read in at least two different ways. In one reading, postmodernism claims that modernity is over and hence we live in a postmodern era; in another view, postmodernism insists that the universalistic claims associated with modernity can no longer be sustained without demurral. And so it goes with the post-secular.[11]

Such a comparison between the progressive history of modernity and secularity can be taken to mean that secularity itself is over and that we therefore live in a post-secular era. Alternatively, the universalistic claims associated with secularization are no longer sustainable. Secularization can no longer be construed as one, single, comprehensive, universalist theory of predetermined religious decline due to the forces of Western modernization. But it is the first proposition, that the age of secularity is surpassed, only to be replaced with the return of religion, that is much in dispute. Many interpret the post-secular to be the end of the secular through the return of religion. This interpretation often comes from religious actors who desire so. Geoghegan writes that "post-secularism is a contested concept that lends itself to ambiguity. It could suggest a deeply antagonistic stance towards secularism, involving the call for a resurgent religiosity, where 'post' really implies 'pre'—a dismantling of the secular culture of the past few."[12]

Kristina Stoeckl points to this idea of the post-secular as a before-and-after "regime change." "Post-secularity becomes, from their point of view, a kind of state of redemption or salvation, a return not *of*, but *to* religion," she argues. "As an outside observer of the Russian Orthodox Church, I often get the impression that leading figures in the church . . . define post-secular society in this sense. They assume that Western secular modernity has run its course, has exhausted itself, has, in fact, become 'post-modern' and 'post-secular,' and is now ready to return to religion."[13] The post-secular in this sense is normative. This understanding of the post-secular as normativity and "regime change" can possibly be seen in the work of Richard John Neuhaus in his 1982 article "Educational Diversity in Post-secular America," where he writes, "We are witnessing the collapse of the 200 year old hegemony of the secular Enlightenment over public discourse."[14]

Stoeckl has taken this possible interpretation of the post-secular as regime change seriously enough to drop the hyphen from *post-secular*, referring only to the *postsecular*, in order to convey her rejection of this time-change scenario.

> Stoeckl defines the post-secular as "a condition of conscious contemporarily/co-existence of religious and secular worldviews. The co-existence of religious and secular worldviews, of religious and secular outlooks on society and politics, of religious and secular modes of understanding one's individual life creates tensions. Post-secularity is a condition of permanent tension."[15]

One crucial work that informs so much of the debates over secularity versus post-secularity is Habermas's "Notes on Post-secular Society." Jürgen Habermas, the last authentic representative of the Frankfurt school and the giant of European philosophy, is largely credited with popularizing the term *post-secular* by employing the term in many of his more recent lectures and articles. Habermas writes that "today, public consciousness in Europe can be described in terms of a 'post-secular society' to the extent that at present it still has to 'adjust itself to the continued existence of religious communities in an increasingly secularized environment.'"[16] Furthermore, the characterization of society in the modern context, according to Habermas, as "post-secular" is commensurate with "a change in consciousness" that derives not so much from shifts in the sensibility of European societies but as a consequence of the general planet-wide transformation we understand as "globalization." Habermas maintains that this change can be ascribed to three general trends: (1) "the broad perception of those global conflicts that are often presented as hinging on religious strife changes public consciousness"; (2) the fact that religious considerations are becoming more an integral part of both national and international public discourse; and (3) an acceleration of immigration through flows across national borders of "guest-workers" as well refugees, especially when these new arrivals are fiercely committed to the values and beliefs they brought from the more traditional societies they left.[17] Hence, the term *post-secular* "refers not only to the fact that religion continues to assert itself in an increasingly secular environment and that society, for the time being, reckons with the continued existence of religious communities."[18]

In addition, Habermas contends that the locution *post-secular* does not simply recognize the enlarged presence in secular societies of peoples with defined religious commitments. It also acknowledges the increasingly "normative" significance of the importance of religion in the public square, even if the social actors who embody this heightened role of the religious are from countries and cultures that previously were not considered a "natural" element of the historical body politic. In a post-secular society, "the modernization of public consciousness" is not automatically equated with a diminution of religious voices. "The return of religion," as Derrida put it, is considered an organic feature of modernization itself. Finally, in a post-secular world both religious and nonreligious people come to acknowledge and respect each other's positions more instinctively.

THE TROUBLE WITH HABERMAS

The problem with Habermas's approach to the post-secular, however, is that it follows the familiar model of the democratic inclusion of cultural—and in this case religious—differences. Habermas simply welcomes "religion" in a manner that the Frankfurt school refused to do for most of their history along with other forms of belief or behavior unique to the big, hypothetical gathering that we conceive as "liberal democracy" at a global level. There is nothing genuinely "critical" about this modus operandi, because Habermas does not recognize the "return of religion" as something fundamental to the shape of the emerging world and to the dynamics of collective meaning that globalization inevitably fosters. The customary liberal conceit is that globalization entails the triumph of Western secular institutions and intellectual norms that gradually infuse the sinews of what should be imagined as a new, international—and broadly secular—"civil society." Nevertheless, as is becoming painfully obvious everywhere on the planet—and especially throughout the "cradle of civilization," to which we give the geographic descriptor *Middle East*—the opposite is the case. Increasingly, religion becomes a powerful driver and a radical, intense commitment that compels people to resist the "pluralistic" demands of Western secular democracy in the name of the one, divine truth that holds their consciousness captive. It is this unbreakable commitment to the one truth that cannot necessarily be distilled into any kind of formal credo, only certain compelling, motivational markers of what Jacques Lacan has called the "symbolic order," which defines generically what we mean by faith.

As Olivier Roy has stressed, the so-called return of religion is wrongly—and often much too dismissively—identified as "fundamentalism." On the contrary, it must be understood as a liberation of the motivating force of religious symbols from culture.[19] And this liberation, in an odd sort of way, also counts as the occasion for the emancipation of faith from what has historically been understood as "religion," that is, as something embedded in distinctive cultural norms and legacies. The return of religion is at once the emancipation of faith as the critical principle and transformative factor amid the new global disorder. In deference to the assumptions of the European Enlightenment, the old critical theory saw religion as a conservative and obscurantist element in sustaining the status quo. According to this view, the "critical" or emancipatory dimension of theory had to be a pure and powerful strain of Enlightenment rationality itself. As Herbert Marcuse held, "pure reason" of the Kantian, or Enlightenment, variety, once it is unleashed, can simultaneously probe, upend and transfigure the prevailing order of both knowledge and existence. But the new critical theory regards not reason but "faith"—the active factor in the return of the "religious," the "force of God"—as performing this very same function instead. A Barth-like "crisis theology," a religiously inspired "negative dialectics" that functions mainly to limit, or annul, the ideological claims and charades behind all schemes of immanent salvation, is in no way adequate for going up against a world in chaos. Generally speaking, crisis theology played a role comparable to so-called deconstructive theological thinking in the last generation. That is, it took a "critical" scalpel to the overdetermined postures and contentions of liberal theology, which saw itself as somehow "constructing" the proper life-worlds and cognitive categories for human beings in what it regarded with a certain naive hubris as a fitting agenda for a new, irreversible "secular age." In an odd respect, crisis theology with its negative dialectics made eminent sense throughout the two-century epoch of a dominant Western secular *imperium* that held colonial sway over much of the planet and its pretensions to a humanistic "civilizing mission." But today's menacing "rough beast" that slouches toward Jerusalem is the very clash of intensified antisecular convictions with its seismic epicenter in the cradle both of civilization and the apocalyptic expectation of the end of all civilizations—namely, the Middle East. At the same time, it is the kind of quasimystical populism and ethnic nationalism with leftward as well as rightward leanings, such as we are witnessing in Europe, that threatens to send the once proud post-Communist, secular international order (what is crudely referred to as its critics mainly as "neoliberalism") as well into a downward tailspin.

The notion of "faith" in this tumultuous venue can no longer be codified simply as a courageous assertion of the traditional "Christian" worldview among multiple, fractious and increasingly intemperate expressions of the new "holy ignorance." Nor can it be some kind of sophisticated "defensive" strategy simply to keep safe and intact a way of being for a certain faith tradition in the maw of the hideous hurricane. The question of the "truth" of faith, which abides at the center of any ongoing project for a critical theology, does *not* turn, *contra* Kierkegaard, on the intensity of the passion by which the content of a conviction is held. Instead, it comes down to the force through which this "critical" factor is expressed and how it can be discerned as reshaping the global order itself. By their fruits you shall know them! In short, it comes down to the "worlding" (as Heidegger would put it) of the very world that faith itself constitutes.

As suggested earlier, the mission of critical theory has always been to salvage the Greek *logos* as a transformative instrument within the chronicle of cultures and societies. Plato's discovery of the original "dialectic" within the practices advanced by, and stories associated with, his teacher Socrates contributed to the first articulation within Western thought of how we might imagine such a "critical" form of *logos*. It was the effort of the first-generation critical theorists both to "deepen" and to empower the Enlightenment concept of *logos* as universal rationality by melding a Marxian criticism of political economy with a radical Kantian "critique of pure reason" and a Nietzschean genealogy of culture, which might erect the scaffolding for the new venture of critical thinking on which we are set to embark today. From a Christian perspective—and even in our multiple universes of pluralized discourses that is the only position from which we can in all seriousness speak "religiously" about a critical theology—the new standpoint of *critique as faith* requires that we discern a *source* of faith from which a critical theology can freely flow. That source consists in the most radical kind of *logos* implied in the affirmation of the *logos* "made flesh."

The Christian conviction that the *logos* ("Word") is "made flesh" is both all-too-familiar and profoundly *not-yet-thought* for any undertaking that might be loosely termed *theology*, especially a critical theology. John 1:14 ("The logos was transformed into flesh and tabernacled in our midst"—*ho logos sarx egenōsen kai eskēnōsen en hēmin*),[20] from which the doctrine of the incarnation derives, opens out a horizon for theological reflection that neither a simple theology of "crisis" nor "negative dialectics" can begin to plumb. As New Testament exegetes have tirelessly pointed out, the Gospel writer in this passage seeks to have his audience freely associate in their minds with the Old Testament narrative of the people of Israel journeying in the wilderness and episodically encountering within the so-called tent of meaning the glorious and incomparable radiance, or Shekinah, of the nameless God who emancipated them from Pharaoh by mysterious might. But, in remembering the new liberator Christ, the author of John's Gospel intimates, those who profess to follow him should rather free associate also with a sense of the powerful work of the *logos* as it was understood in Hellenistic society, as the vigor of critical reason. Hence the "rationality" of any Christian theology is inextricably bound up with the misidentified "irrationality" of the critical *logos* as embroiled in the very messiness of *sarx*, or "flesh." Such a presumed "unreason," however, betrays a more powerful critical function of word/reason/logos that once and for all historicizes as well as "globalizes" in an even "messier" manner. Ultimately, it manifests not only as a Hegelian "reason" in history but also as a "theo-rationality" of embodied encounter and conflicted involvement of selves with others, a kaleidoscopic kind of interactivity that the propositional logic undergirding conventional philosophical inquiry cannot even pretend to comprehend or penetrate. This kind of rationality amounts to a *semiotic rationality*, which the "religious" expresses, a rationality of sign-processes that express this kind of force-generating singularity out of which emerges the kind of intimate relationality embodied in Genesis 2 with the creation of man and woman as the "image of God." To improve on Hegel's famous principle that the "rational" is always real, we can say that the rational is ultimately real because it is at once deeply *relational*.

Biblical scholarship has debated for many generations the differing nuances of the word *sarx* in the Scriptures. The word varies significantly in different contexts, especially when Paul gets hold of it to make his case against Pharisaic Judaism in the book of Romans. But its implications are even more complex as well as staggering in the so-called prologue to John's Gospel. The *logos* of the ancient Stoic philosophers, whose intuitions John may have subtly appropriated by way of his reading of the Jewish philosopher Philo of Alexander, can be characterized as the creative, ordering principle of the entire cosmos. The Stoic *logos* is closer to the Enlightenment concept of "right reason" (*orthos logos*), which Max Horkheimer often mentions. The Johannine *logos*, however, is not an "orthodox" *logos*. Nor is it the "Word of God" as opposed to the "Word of Man," as Barth would have it. It is more closely akin to what contemporary theologian John Milbank terms the "Word made strange."

But this "strangeness" emanates from its radical historical and existential contingency, the frailty and unpredictability of events, as the term *sarx* implies, out of which the singularity of the Badiouan event appears. It is, at the same time, the singularity of Žižek's fractured subjectivity that spurs the militancy of the new "Christian"/political collective. The "incarnate" *logos* is such an eventuality in its own right. Indeed, it is the Event that redefines and redirects all events. It is not "dialectical" so much as it is dialogical. It operates critically within the space of all our fractured subjectivities as the *logos* that meets us constantly, as the philosopher Emmanuel Levinas says, in the face of the other, in the give-and-take of our embodied otherness to each other that the ancients called the "flesh." The genuinely critical dimension of such a theology of the enfleshed *logos* lies in its very "e-vental" contingency, meaning that it meets us in the "tent of meeting" that is our very own skin, and the skin of others. It is Christ made real to us through others, through the miracle of alterity. It is the *logos* that becomes the "premise" for the criticism of all those premises that reduce others to commodities or expendables, to systems of economic calculation and the castration of people's productive potentials, totalitarian impulses to eliminate dissent and difference, identitarian regimes that distance and exclude all those who cannot be enfolded within their imagined communities of the same. It is the *logos* of a truly "critical" critical theology.

GLOBALIZATION AS CONTEXT FOR CRITICAL THEOLOGY

But how exactly does this new kind of theo-*logos* leverage the context of globalization with an edge that earlier critical theory did not? Up through the nineteenth century and into the first decades of the twentieth century, Marxism itself, out of which critical theory emerged, had always assumed that the globalization of capital as the world industrialized was the determinative setting for the prophesied emancipation of the workers of the world. Eschewing what it considered a rigid Marxist orthodoxy that had sprung up after World War I with the Third International, or Comintern, which quickly become an extension of the Stalinist regime in Moscow, the earlier critical theorists asserted in effect that emancipation must first take place in the realm of culture, since the advent of mass media had provided the "ruling classes" with an unprecedented means of imposing a "false consciousness" on the international proletariat. Liberation, they asserted, must be as much cognitive as it is material. But such liberation could only occur once the conditions for enslavement were perceived no longer as local but as global.

Nowadays, as in former eras, there is a certain amount of posturing and grandstanding about economic oppression and inequality, often resulting in half-baked proposals about combating the new global regime of virtualized and highly financialized capital that has come to be known imprecisely as "neoliberalism." But the "psycho-spiritual" dimensions of both the nature of such oppression and the trajectories of emancipation are all too frequently shunted aside. Just as classical critical theory tackled these kinds of issues that orthodox forms of political radicalism had dismissed as inconsequential, so a new critical theology is summoned as well to address them squarely and consistently. One contemporary figure who is not routinely classified as part of the "new critical theory," but whose work has momentous ramifications for supplying the "global" component to an emergent critical theology, is Ulrich Beck. I briefly discussed his contributions to the debates over post-secularism, but we also must regard him as providing some real heft to the idea of critical theology in a genuinely global context.

Essentially Beck argues that the newest wave of globalization in the last quarter century has brought about what he terms a different "meta-game of world politics" than what prevailed throughout much of the twentieth century. With a different "meta-game" comes different rules of power and the political exercise of dominion and sovereignty. The contestants in the older game, according to Beck, were nation-states and their official representants. The players in the new game are global entrepreneurs, financiers and culturemakers. They also include nonstate actors who disrupt the rules of the game—in other words, "terrorists." Beck describes the theoretical elements of this novel meta-game as a "new critical theory with cosmopolitan intent." Beck, in fact, prefers the term *cosmopolitanism* to *globalization* to denominate the mingling of peoples and the confluence of cultures and economies. According to Beck, "The cosmopolitan question is: what is your attitude towards the otherness of others?"[21] Cosmopolitanism itself means "the acknowledgment of difference."[22] Beck

distinguishes cosmopolitanism from multiculturalism. Whereas multiculturalism "implies . . . an essentialist identity and rivalry between cultures" and a person is a "mere epiphenomenon of their culture and society,"[23] cosmopolitanism entails "acknowledging the otherness of those
who are culturally different."[24]

What I have termed the "dialogical" *logos* of a new critical theology,
the procedural "theo-logic" that emanates from the "axiomatic" *logos* of
the Word made flesh, therefore becomes the only kind of "critical" rationality that can successfully navigate the topography of intersecting power
relations that have left the political architecture of the nation-state historically in the lurch. We are all wayfarers, and at the same time we are
all "stripped naked"—so to speak—when we come face-to-face and communicate with each other in our itinerant voyagings and concurrences.
A new, global critical theology would therefore be cosmopolitan in Beck's
pivotal sense. It would not be some overreaching and disinterested sur-
veillance of vast and turbid transnational hoi polloi. The question of
identity in such a global critical theology gives pride of place to the recognition and reciprocal incorporation of difference into the formation
of a thousand engaged "critical" subjectivities arising from the inescapable
intersubjectivity of a world without national borders and static cultural
boundaries for which the venerable science of "politics," even at the international level, becomes meaningless.

By the same token, the potential confusion of any critical theology with
standard political theologies has to be cleared up. It is of course a no-brainer
that the idea of the "political," on which any political theology is based,
centers on the shifting concept of the *polis*, or territorially defined self-
regulating community (in the modern era, the "nation-state"). But a global
critical theology, while taking seriously the national *polis* as the epicenter of
governance, administration and "policymaking," looks beyond both the
structures and strictures of the *political* to essay the question of human
emancipation in its rawest kind of contemporary "situatedness." This
question of human emancipation not en masse but *secundum propriam
cuiusque alium* (according to each different person), therefore, becomes

Beck's true "cosmopolitan" question. It becomes not so much an ethics of engagement, but a theory of how *I* deal *transcendentally* with the present reality of the other in a very real and quotidian sense. In short, it is the "good Samaritan's question," what Derrida terms "cosmopolitan" hospitality.

That question has a different "transcendental" objective than what remains standard for political theology. The very notion of a "political theology," which has undergone a number of elaborations and fluctuations since Carl Schmitt coined the word in its modern sense almost a century ago, amounts to the realization that the ongoing formulation of active political ideas cannot be separated from transcendental arguments, particularly when it comes to the enunciation of moral imperatives such as human equality and the promotion of human rights. Political theology discerns deeply the "force of God" behind the *force of politics,* as I argue elsewhere.[25] And it constructs its analysis and orchestrates its positions around this important controlling assumption. Political theology by and large is a normative discipline, although descriptive procedures and protocols invariably and incessantly come into play in the elaboration of what might broadly be described as a kind of *transcendental political theory*, while invoking the term *transcendental* in something of the manner it was used from Kant through Husserl.

A critical theology, on the other hand, harbors its own "transcendental" method, probing further than any standard approach into the generative dynamics of even those "religious" realities stalking behind the masks of politics. And we find, not surprisingly, that these religious realities are not only the imperative of transcendent loyalty—or what Levinas terms "infinite responsibility"—but the *cosmopolitan challenge* to meet the other in his or her global situatedness. We might refer to its modus operandi as not only "meta-theological" but also *meta-transcendental*, a transcendental "deduction" of transcendence as a whole. At the same time, a critical theology is in no way merely "reductive" toward, nor "suspicious" of, the structures it mobilizes for its special "diagnostic" reading of various cultural assemblages, as well as the transcendental background of social, economic and political phenomena. A critical theology, as opposed to a critical theory, identifies and peers into what Derrida and his compiler Gil Anidjar would term "acts of religion" in accordance with what might be labeled a *driving theory* of the religious itself. A critical theology is therefore the discourse that unfurls this driving theory. It is the theory of how we respond to alterity in accordance with transcendental requirements.

The need for such a driving theory is posed by the reality of globalization itself. Roy makes the case in *Holy Ignorance* for such a "critical theology," because the very Enlightenment paradigm of what Derrida himself has called a "religion without religion" is becoming obsolete. Religious positivities in the historical sense, Roy insists, are inherently and "phenomenologically" bound up with recognized cultural formations. But today's religion is essentially *cultureless*, especially as the effects of global connectivity and communications systems rapidly erase the "traditional" substance behind the numberless and often commodified spiritual practices and arbitrary, spiritual "markers" (e.g., pop Kabbalism for New Agers, or "worship bands" at African mosques) that are everywhere in evidence from Britain to Bangladesh. Since these new sorts of spiritual ephemera, or the more austere types of new, stripped-down religious "fundamentalisms," all have the force of conviction, if not fanaticism, behind them, they all emanate from an undefined mood of what we ourselves might dub "universalism without universality," a general condition Roy characterizes as the new "holy ignorance." The prompt for a critical theology in a global context is offered by Roy. "Neither philosophy nor culture, but a constant reminder of a transcendence, irreducible to the material world, and on which the world order is founded: what should be religion's place in the social order."[26] Or, better yet, what should be the "theological" resources on which we draw the critical analyses and insights to lay bare with a certain discursive sophistication this "constant reminder of a transcendence"? That constant reminder, as we have seen, is the "other," emblazoned in the great historical reminder that *ho logos sarx egeneto* (the *logos* became flesh). The "enfleshed" *logos* is always the *logos* for us that subsists in dynamic, passionate relation to us (Jn 1:14 NIV).

While "theological" pursuits in the last half century have often focused on explicitly Christian, quasi-Christian or crypto-Christian themes that still bear the mark of what is nowadays regarded often as a privileged and "hegemonic" Western point of view, the so-called *study of religion*—or "religious studies"—has bracketed almost obsessively both the theoretical and theological tasks by focusing, sometimes exclusively, on selective anthropological and historical particularities that satisfy the unstated secularist criteria for what still remains a "Eurocentric" method of inquiry. Likewise, the default status for those more savvy scholars who acknowledge the deep bias behind what is glibly passed off as the "objective" investigation of all things "religious" is a kind of unreflective deference to confessional accounts of what religious or theological statements are supposed to mean, especially when these accounts constitute the "discourse of the other." A good example is how many religious scholars will at once allow one of Roy's hypothetical "deculturated" Muslim speakers to have their full and unchallenged say while automatically dismissing a present-day evangelical or Pentecostal testimony as somehow tainted with the obvious biases of the "dominant culture." A global critical theology, however, would seek to facilitate the deconstruction of the ever-seductive Western "myth of objectivity" as well as the spurious "insider/outsider" dichotomy in which present-day scholarship has trapped itself. And it would obliterate once and for all the notion that emancipation is nothing more than exchanging "dominant" narratives for "excluded" ones." In fact, "excluded" narratives can only claim a privileged voice to the extent that they manifest the universal and transcendent voice of the "I AM" that is often located in what Beck dubs narratives of "inclusive difference," or radical intersubjectivity. If the singularity of the "critical" insight does not lead to a new and more compelling universality of truth with this twist it has no right to such a privilege.

THE TASK OF A GLOBAL CRITICAL THEOLOGY

At the same time, a global critical theology will go where no probe has necessarily gone before in essaying a genealogy of the political signs and tokens that populate our habits of thought. It will also focus on the *politico-economic* dimensions of culture where what we term the "religious" has profoundly evident and compelling theological implications. It would also confront the illusory Hobson's choice of descriptive rigor versus transcendental normativity, a habit of mind that regrettably has lodged like some alien genome in our own operative *epistēmē* since Kant first distinguished between "theoretical" and "practical" reason. For the first time in the evolution of contemporary learning and letters, a critical theology, therefore, would strategically merge the theory of religion with the "theological" constitution of all transcendental inquiry, which the persistence of the religious factor in the world we experience every day pushes inexorably on us. It would not be independent of a political theology. Indeed, it would serve to ground it in richer and ever more "critical" ways.

But what makes critical theology ultimately "critical," as I have underscored, is what gives it that very searching, if not "abysmal," and *discerning* (as the etymology of the word itself insists) force that stands behind it, the force that penetrates into the diffused and interconnected subjectivities that cry out for recognition amid a planet in crisis. Such a force itself—the force of God—is the outtake of the Event that was only hazily discerned on a spring afternoon two millennia ago, at a site for executing criminals known as Golgotha, "the Place of the Skull," outside the city of Jerusalem in that turbulent region known as the Middle East. In that event, the event of the incarnation, which includes not only Good Friday but also Easter morning, for the first time in history God became *Emmanuel*, God "with us" and "for us." With that event a seemingly cosmic "crisis" takes place, as signified in the tearing of the veil of the temple, the storm and the earthquake. But the crisis is also cultural and social at the same time. An entirely new *critical discernment* about the nature and destiny of humankind, not to mention the general order of things, once and for all is untethered. The event is not fully disclosed; it is still on its way, yet remaining to be fully disclosed. The early Christian expectation of a parousia, or "fullness of presence," of the Christ event itself, a return or "yet to come," remains still with us.

A critical theology is not some glorified type of Christian social ethics, nor does it belong to the rhythmic cadence of failed political enthusiasms and reactive, "revolutionary" follies that litter the abandoned battlefields of collective memory. A critical theology does not make merely one more wearisome, moralistic or outraged gesture toward reminding us that there is injustice somewhere out there as we speak, or that we need to do something—or do "anything"—in order to appease discreetly our consciences about having it better together than we are comfortable with, or to feel somehow in our anguished impotence that we have been amply aroused to "make a difference." A critical theology amounts to the most vigorous and encyclopedic deployment of the resources of a Christian faith commitment that seeks, like the critical theory of old, to comprehend and dissect, to know and be prepared to act at the same time. "It is not enough for theory," as Baudrillard contends, "to describe and analyse; it must itself be an event in the universe it describes. In order to do this theory must partake of and become the acceleration of this logic. It must tear itself from all referents and take pride only in the future."[27]

Such a future is truly what in theological parlance we would characterize as "eschatological," which is both immanent and transcendent in the same breath. The age of the personalized and privatized Reformation-style evangel is over. The curtain has come down on Western Christianity as one skillfully orchestrated "Jesus show" that pretends to be for its viewers all at once intellectually stimulating, therapeutically effective, emotionally satisfying, morally uplifting and relentlessly entertaining. As the sometimes mad playwright Antonin Artaud once observed, the "show" must not only go on but also now move into the streets, where the actors and the audience coalesce into one mobilized mass that changes the scene once and for all. Artaud called this transformation of the "play" into event the "theater of cruelty," a trope that to this day remains puzzling to his readers. Much of current academic theology, not to mention avant-garde political theory, has become nevertheless low-key theater of the absurd. A real sense of crisis is slowly beginning to take hold. With a nod to Heidegger, we might be bold enough to proclaim that *only a critical theology can save us.*

Thus we must ask ourselves what such a "saving" form of the theological reminds us about. Following Artaud's tacit understanding of the
"theoretical" as a mode of the "theatrical," or any presumed "spectacle" as
a type of *participatory performance*, we may further pose the most "critical"
question that stalks the history of critical theory—how can we transition
from mere theory to transformative praxis? How does one move from
interpreting to changing the world, from analyzing the conditions of *un-
freedom* to emancipating living human beings from their circumstances
of oppression? Certainly the very aims of both critical theory and an in-
cipient critical theology are suggested in the very saying of Jesus, "You will
know the truth, and the truth will set you free" (Jn 8:32 NIV). A critical
theology turns the critical-theoretical perspective of the Christian faith
itself into liberating practice. But it is at the same time a practice power-
fully informed by both a personal and a corporate sense that one is acting
in accordance, as Badiou would phrase it, with the singularity of the
event—in this case the Christ event that is both alpha and omega, not just
ontological but also eschatological, within the same zone of awareness.
Badiou understands this "fidelity" to the event as a stance of militancy.

The term *militant,* with the same etymology as *military,* can naturally
on the one hand connote armed struggle. But it has a secondary and more
pertinent meaning as well—persistent and even "aggressive" adherence to
an overarching cause. The ancient Christian notion of the "church militant,"
that is, a collective agency driven by the secular mandate of Jesus himself
at the Great Commission to his disciples to go to "the ends of the earth" to
usher in the *eschaton*, looms large for us at this particular juncture in
history. To respond to the commission of critical theology amid a world in
chaos is not so much, as the Jewish philosopher Spinoza limned it, the
"intellectual love of God," but an *intelligent fidelity* to the Event of God that
summons us in telling, but often highly ambiguous, ways at a moment's
notice. Only a critical theology can "save us" in this connection because
what makes it "critical" in the first place is the very "risk" we take for the
coming kingdom of God. Beck tells us that the globo-cosmopolitan world
in which we are increasingly enmeshed can be described as a "risk society"

where the security of place and the security of clear and evident conviction themselves are mirages that easily vanish from our sight as we trudge through this new, cruel "desert of the real." Jesus himself commanded that we be ready to risk all for his sake. A critical theology, therefore, can guide us in delineating how high the stakes are, and why it is worth risking our worlds as well as our lives for them.

Notes

PREFACE

[1]Friedrich Nietzsche, *The Gay Science*, trans. Thomas Common (North Chelmsford, MA: Courier, 2012), 90.

CHAPTER 1: GLOBALIZATION AND THE EMERGENCE OF A NEW CRITICAL THEORY FOR THE AGE OF CRISIS

[1]Habermas's most important works are as follows: Jürgen Habermas, *The Theory of Communicative Action*, vol. 1, *Reason and the Rationalization of Society*, trans. Thomas McCarthy (Boston: Beacon, 1984); Habermas, *The Theory of Communicative Action*, vol. 2, *Lifeworld and System: A Critique of Functionalist Reason*, trans. Thomas McCarthy (Boston: Beacon, 1987).

[2]Horkheimer's chief works are, in addition to those he coauthored with Adorno, Max Horkheimer, *Critique of Instrumental Reason*, trans. Matthew J. O'Connell et al. (New York: Verso, 2012); Horkheimer, *Eclipse of Reason* (New York: Continuum, 2004).

[3]For Benjamin, see *inter alia* his books Walter Benjamin, *Illuminations: Essays and Reflections*, ed. Hannah Arendt, trans. Harry Zohn (New York: Schocken, 2007); Benjamin, *The Origin of German Tragic Drama*, trans. John Osborne (New York: Verso, 1998).

[4]Marcuse was very influential on the social thought of the 1960s. His major books include Herbert Marcuse, *Reason and Revolution: Hegel and the Rise of Social Theory* (London: Routledge and Kegan Paul, 1955); Marcuse, *Counterrevolution and Revolt* (Boston: Beacon, 1972); Marcuse, *Eros and Civilization: A Philosophical Inquiry into Freud* (Boston: Beacon, 1974); Marcuse, *Essays in Critical Theory*, trans. Jeremy J. Shapiro (London: MayFly, 2009); Marcuse, *One-Dimensional Man: Studies in the Ideology of Advanced Industrial Society*, Routledge Classics (New York: Routledge, 2002); and Marcuse, *The Aesthetic Dimension: Toward a Critique of Marxist Aesthetics* (Boston: Beacon, 1978).

[5]Erich Fromm was better known as a popular writer than as an academic theorist. His most important work, so far as it reflects the agenda of the Frankfurt school, was Fromm, *Escape from Freedom* (New York: Holt, 1994).

[6]Some other important writings of the Frankfurt school include Theodor W. Adorno, *Negative Dialectics*, trans. E. B. Ashton (New York: Bloomsbury, 2014); Adorno, *Minima Moralia: Reflections from Damaged Life*, trans. E. F. N. Jephcott (New York: Verso, 2005); Walter Benjamin, *The Work of Art in the Age of Its Technical Reproducibility and Other Writings on Media*, ed. Michael W. Jennings et al., trans. Edmund Jephcott et al. (Cambridge, MA: Harvard University Press, 2008); Alfred Schmidt, *The Concept of Nature in Marx*, trans. Ben Fowkes (New York: New Left Books, 1971); Alfred Sohn-Roethel, *Intellectual and Manual Labor: A Critique of Epistemology*, trans. Martin Sohn-Roethel (London: Macmillan, 1978).

[7]Jean-Jacques Rousseau, *On The Social Contract*, trans. G. D. H. Cole (Mineola, NY: Dover, 2003), 1.

[8]Max Horkheimer, "Traditional and Critical Theory," in *Critical Sociology: Selected Readings*, ed. Paul Connerton (New York: Penguin, 1978), 219.

[9]The so-called new critical theory encompasses a vast range of writers in theorists in uncounted disciplines in both the humanities and social sciences. However, we can compile a list of some of the most prominent authors and their works. They include Giorgio Agamben, *Homo Sacer: Sovereign Power and Bare Life*, trans. Daniel Heller-Roazen (Stanford: Stanford University Press, 1998); Agamben, *Language and Death: The Place of Negativity*, trans. Karen E. Pinkus with Michael Hardt (Minneapolis: University of Minnesota Press, 1991); Alain Badiou, *Deleuze: The Clamor of Being*, trans. Louise Burchill (Minneapolis: University of Minnesota Press, 1999); Badiou, *Ethics: An Essay on the Understanding of Evil*, trans. Peter Hallward (New York: Verso, 2001); Badiou, *Infinite Thought: Truth and the Return to Philosophy*, trans. Oliver Feltham and Justin Clemens (New York: Continuum, 2004); Badiou, *Logics of Worlds: Being and Event II*, trans. Alberto Toscano (New York: Continuum, 2009); Badiou, *Manifesto for Philosophy* (Albany: State University of New York Press, 1999); Badiou, *Metapolitics*, trans. Jason Barker (New York: Verso, 2005); Badiou, *St. Paul: The Foundations of Universalism*, trans. Ray Brassier (Stanford: Stanford University Press, 2003); Badiou, *The Communist Hypothesis*, trans. David Macey and Steve Corcoran (New York: Verso, 2010); Badiou, *Theory of the Subject*, trans. Bruno Bosteels (New York: Continuum, 2009); Jean Baudrillard, *Simulacra and Simulation*, trans. Sheila Faria Glaser (Ann Arbor: University of Michigan Press, 1994); Baudrillard, *Symbolic Exchange and Death*, trans. Iain Hamilton Grant (London: Sage, 1993); Gilles Deleuze, *Difference and Repetition*, trans. Paul Patton (New York: Columbia University Press, 1994); Gilles

Deleuze and Felix Guattari, *Anti-Oedipus: Capitalism and Schizophrenia*, trans. Robert Hurley, Mark Seem and Helen R. Lane (New York: Penguin, 1977); Jacques Derrida, *Of Grammatology*, trans. Gayatri Chakravorty Spivak (Baltimore: Johns Hopkins University Press, 1997); Derrida, *The Gift of Death and Literature in Secret*, trans. David Wills (Chicago: University of Chicago Press, 2008); Antonio Gramsci, *Pre-prison Writings*, ed. Richard Bellamy, trans. Virginia Cox (Cambridge: Cambridge University Press, 1994); *Prison Notebooks*, vols. 1-3, ed. and trans. Joseph A. Buttigieg (New York: Columbia University Press, 2011); Luce Irigaray, *Speculum of the Other Woman*, trans. Gillian C. Gill (Ithaca, NY: Cornell University Press, 1985); Irigaray, *This Sex Which Is Not One*, trans. Catherine Porter with Carolyn Burke (Ithaca, NY: Cornell University Press, 1985); Julia Kristeva, *In the Beginning Was Love: Psychoanalysis and Faith*, trans. Arthur Goldhammer (New York: Columbia University Press, 1987); Kristeva, *Powers of Horror: An Essay on Abjection*, trans. Leon S. Roudiez (New York: Columbia University Press, 1982); Jacques Lacan, *The Seminar of Jacques Lacan*, book 7, *The Ethics of Psychoanalysis, 1959–1960*, ed. Jacques-Alain Miller, trans. Dennis Porter (New York: Norton, 1992); Lacan, *The Seminar of Jacques Lacan*, book 20, *On Feminine Sexuality, The Limits of Love and Knowledge, 1972–1973*, ed. Jacques-Alain Miller, trans. Bruce Fink (New York: Norton, 1999); Georg Lukács, *History and Class Consciousness: Studies in Marxist Dialectics*, trans. Rodney Livingstone (Cambridge, MA: MIT Press, 1971); Lukács, *Lenin: A Study on the Unity of His Thought*, trans. Nicholas Jacobs (New York: Verso, 2009); Jacques Rancière, *Proletarian Nights: The Worker's Dream in Nineteenth-Century France*, trans. John Drury (New York: Verso, 2012); Rancière, *The Ignorant Schoolmaster: Five Lessons in Intellectual Emancipation*, trans. Kristin Ross (Stanford: Stanford University Press, 1999).

[10]Such leading institutions include, among others, the University of California at Berkeley, the University of California at Irvine, the University of Washington, Northwestern University, Cornell University and the University of Denver.

[11]See Badiou, *Logics of Worlds*.

[12]Alain Badiou, *The Rebirth of History: Times of Riots and Uprisings*, trans. Gregory Elliott (New York: Verso, 2012).

[13]Philip Jenkins, *The Great and Holy War: How World War I Became a Religious Crusade* (New York: HarperCollins, 2014), 2.

[14]See Andreas Vrahimis, *Encounters Between Analytic and Continental Philosophy* (New York: Palgrave Macmillan, 2013), 34.

[15]For a good general discussion of the Bultmann-Heidegger relationship, see William D. Dennison, *The Young Bultmann: Context for His Understanding of God, 1884–1925* (New York: Peter Lang, 2008).

[16]Rudolf Bultmann, *Interpreting Faith for the Modern Era*, ed. Roger A. Johnson (Minneapolis: Fortress, 1991), 45.

[17]Ibid., 48 (emphasis added).

[18]The relationship between Bultmann and Heidegger is sometimes contested by scholars. The early Bultmann was decidedly influenced by Wilhelm Hermann, as Christopher Chalamet argues. See Chalamet, *Dialectical Theologians: Wilhelm Hermann, Karl Barth, and Rudolf Bultmann* (Zürich: Theologisher Verlag, 2005). David Congdon argues that the thought of Johannes Weiss is even more important. See Congdon, *The Mission of Demythologizing: Rudolf Bultmann's Dialectical Theology* (Minneapolis: Fortress, 2015). It is quite evident, however, that Bultmann's later program of hermeneutical theology grounded in the concept of *Existenz* was drawn from his relationship with Heidegger at Marburg, which commenced in 1923. In an autobiographical essay Bultmann wrote, "The work of existential philosophy, which I came to know through Martin Heidegger, has become of decisive significance for me. I found in it the conceptuality in which to speak adequately of human existence and therefore also of the existence of the believer." Rudolf Bultmann, *Existence and Faith: Shorter Writings of Rudolf Bultmann*, ed. and trans. Schubert Ogden (New York: World, 1961), 258. For an analysis of Bultmann's debt to Heidegger, see also John Williams, *Martin Heidegger's Philosophy of Religion* (Waterloo, ON: Wilfred Laurier University Press, 1977); Leroy Miller and Stanley Grenz, eds., *Fortress Introduction to Contemporary Theologies* (Minneapolis: Fortress, 1998), 43.

[19]Karl Barth, *The Word of God and the Word of Man*, trans. Douglas Horton (Gloucester, MA: Peter Smith, 1978), 80.

[20]Gary Dorrien, *Theology Without Weapons: The Barthian Revolt in Modern Theology* (Louisville, KY: Westminster John Knox, 2000), 57

[21]See Chalamet, *Dialectical Theologians*.

[22]The "emancipatory" mission of critical theory has had wide implications for present-day progressive movements. For example, the larger movement during the 1990s to embed "critical thinking" in the curriculum of both K-12 and higher education can be traced to the ideas of the Frankfurt school. A significant article in this connection is Carol A. Morgaine, "Enlightenment for Emancipation: A Critical Theory of Self-Formation," *Family Relations* 43, no. 3 (1994): 325-35. We can also see critical theory in general applied to the issues of globalization, though not in the large way that this book essays. See, for instance, Christopher Farrands, "Critical Theory in Global Political Economy: Critique? Knowledge? Emancipation?," *Capital and Class* 29 (Spring 2005): 43-61.

[23]Marcuse, *Reason and Revolution*, 123.

[24]According to *The New World Encylopedia* online, dialectical materialism is "the philosophical expression of Marxism and Marxism-Leninism. The name refers to the notion that Marxism is a materialist worldview with a dialectical method. It was developed by Karl Marx and Frederick Engels in the mid-late eighteenth century and further elaborated by later Marxist theorists. Dialectical materialism holds that the world, including human beings, is 'matter in motion' and that progress occurs through struggle. It follows the Hegelian principle of the philosophy of history, namely the development of the thesis into its antithesis, which is in turn superseded by a synthesis that conserves aspects of the thesis and the antithesis while at the same time abolishing them." http://www.newworldencyclopedia.org/entry /Dialectical_materialism.

[25]Definition from *The Encyclopedia Brittanica* online: "In the ethics of the 18th-century German philosopher Immanuel Kant, founder of critical philosophy, a moral law that is unconditional or absolute for all agents, the validity or claim of which does not depend on any ulterior motive or end. 'Thou shalt not steal,' for example, is categorical as distinct from the hypothetical imperatives associated with desire, such as 'Do not steal if you want to be popular.' For Kant there was only one such categorical imperative, which he formulated in various ways. 'Act only according to that maxim by which you can at the same time will that it should become a universal law' is a purely formal or logical statement and expresses the condition of the rationality of conduct rather than that of its morality, which is expressed in another Kantian formula: 'So act as to treat humanity, whether in your own person or in another, always as an end, and never as only a means.'" http://www.britannica.com/topic/categorical-imperative.

[26]In my own work *Moral Action, God, and History in the Thought of Immanuel Kant* (Missoula, MT: Scholars Press, 1975), I made the deep connection between critical theory, Marxian use of Hegel and Kant's own ethics and political philosophy.

[27]Herbert Marcuse, "Philosophy and Critical Theory," in *Critical Theory and Society: A Reader*, ed. by Stephen E. Bonner and Douglas MacKay Kellner (New York: Routledge, 1989), 63.

[28]Agnes Heller, "Habermas and Marxism," in *Habermas: Critical Debates*, ed. John B. Thompson and David Held (Cambridge MA: MIT Press, 1982), 22.

[29]Ibid., 25.

[30]Horkheimer, "Traditional and Critical Theory," 188-89.

[31]Ibid., 203.

[32]Martin Jay, *The Dialectical Imagination: A History of the Frankfurt School and the Institute of Social Research 1923–1950* (Boston: Little, Brown, 1973), 81.

Chapter 2: The Need for a New Critical Theology

[1] See Edward S. Ellis and Charles F. Horne, *The Story of the Greatest Nations: From the Dawn of History to the Twentieth Century* (New York: Francis R. Niglutsch, 1906), 907.

[2] Martin Heidegger, *What Is Called Thinking?*, trans. J. Glenn Gray (New York: HarperCollins, 1976), 6.

[3] Hannah Arendt, *The Life of the Mind—Thinking—Willing* (New York: Harvest, 1978), 4.

[4] See Ola Sigrudson, *Theology and Marxism in Žižek and Eagleton: A Conspiracy of Hope* (New York: Palgrave Macmillan, 2012).

[5] See Mark Lilla, *The Stillborn God: Religion, Politics, and the Modern West* (New York: Knopf, 2007).

[6] See the opening sections of Carl Raschke, *Force of God: Political Theology and the Crisis of Liberal Democracy* (New York: Columbia University Press, 2015).

[7] Max Horkheimer, *Critical Theory: Selected Essays,* trans. Matthew J. O'Connell et al. (New York: Continuum, 1992), 42.

[8] See Peter Strawson, *The Bounds of Sense: An Essay on Kant's Critique of Pure Reason* (New York: Routledge, 2002).

[9] John L. Austin, *How to Do Things with Words* (Oxford: Clarendon, 1962), 5.

[10] Jürgen Habermas, *The Theory of Communicative Action,* vol. 1, *Reason and the Rationalization of Society,* trans. Thomas McCarthy (Boston: Beacon, 1984), 280.

[11] Joseph Cardinal Ratzinger and Jürgen Habermas, *The Dialectics Of Secularization* (San Francisco: Ignatius, 2010), 23.

[12] Ibid.

[13] Jürgen Habermas et al., *An Awareness of What Is Missing: Faith and Reason in a Post-secular Age* (Cambridge: Polity, 2010), Kindle edition, locations 356-59.

[14] Ibid., 389-91.

Chapter 3: From Political Theology to a Global Critical Theology

[1] Jacob Taubes, "Theology and Political Theory," *Social Research* 22 (Spring 1955): 57.

[2] Ibid.

[3] Adam Kotsko, "Genealogy and Political Theology: On Method in Agamben's *The Kingdom and the Glory*," *Political Theology* 14 (2013): 107-14.

[4] Creston Davis, "Editorial Introduction: Political Theology—The Continental Shift," *Political Theology* 11 (2010): 5-14.

[5] See Claude Lefort, "The Permanence of the Theo-Political?," in *Political Theologies: Public Religions in a Post-secular World,* ed. Hent de Vries and Lawrence E. Sullivan (New York: Fordham University Press, 2006), 148-87.

[6]See especially Carl Raschke, *Postmodernism and the Revolution in Religious Theory: Toward a Semiotics of the Event* (Charlottesville: University of Virginia Press, 2012).

[7]David Ohana, "Ambiguous Messianism: The Political Theology of Martin Buber," *Religion Compass* 5, no. 1 (2011): 50.

[8]Hent de Vries, "Introduction: Before, Around and Beyond the Theologico-Political," in de Vries and Sullivan, *Political Theologies*, 25. See also Francis Schüssler Fiorena, "Political Theology," in *New Catholic Encyclopedia*, 2nd ed. (Detroit: Gale, 2003), 11:460.

[9]Leo Strauss, "How to Study Spinoza's 'Theologico-Political Treatise,'" *Proceedings of the American Academy for Jewish Research* 17 (1947–1948): 69.

[10]Richard Shorten, "Political Theology, Political Religion and Secularisation," *Political Studies Review* 8 (2010): 182.

[11]Carl Schmitt, *Political Theology: Four Chapters on the Concept of Sovereignty*, trans. George Schwab (Cambridge, MA: MIT Press, 1985), 36.

[12]Olivier Roy, *Secularism Confronts Islam* (Cambridge: Cambridge University Press, 2013), 40.

[13]See Émile Durkheim, *The Elementary Forms of Religious Life*, trans. Karen Elise Fields (New York: Free Press, 1995).

[14]Roger Scruton, "Political Theology," in *The Palgrave Macmillan Dictionary of Political Thought*, 3rd ed. (New York: Palgrave Macmillan, 2007), 533.

[15]Banu Bargu, *After Secular Law*, ed. Winnifred Sullivan, Robert Yelle and Mateo Taussig-Rubbo (Stanford: Stanford University Press, 2011), 142-43.

[16]Mark Lilla, *The Stillborn God: Religion, Politics, and the Modern West* (New York: Knopf, 2007), 112.

[17]Paul Kahn, *Political Theology: Four New Chapters on the Concept of Sovereignty* (New York: Columbia University Press, 2013).

[18]Rainer Bucher, *Hitler's Theology: A Study in Political Religion*, trans. Rebecca Pohl, ed. Michael Hoelzl (New York: Continuum, 2011), xv.

[19]Michael Hoelzl, "Political Theology and Its Discontents," in *Future of Political Theology: Religious and Theological Perspectives*, ed. Peter Losonczi and Aakash Singh (Farnham, UK: Ashgate, 2012), 23.

[20]Ibid.

[21]Johann Baptist Metz, *Theology of the World*, trans. W. Glen-Doepel (New York: Herder, 1971), 110 (emphasis original).

[22]Ibid.

[23]Jürgen Moltmann, "Political Theology," *Theology Today* 28 (1971): 8.

[24]Ibid., 15

[25]Graham Hammill and Julia Reinhard Lupton, eds., with a postscript by Etienne

Balibar, *Political Theology and Early Modernity* (Chicago: University of Chicago Press, 2012), 1.

[26]Michael Jon Kessler, "Difference, Resemblance, Dialogue: Some Goals for a Comparative Political Theology in a Plural Age," *Political Theology for a Plural Age* (New York: Oxford University Press, 2013), 134.

[27]Elizabeth Phillips, *Political Theology: A Guide for the Perplexed* (New York: T&T Clark, 2012), 155.

[28]De Vries, "Introduction," 25.

[29]Graham Ward, foreword to Losonczi and Aakash Singh, *Future of Political Theology*, xiii.

[30]Phillips, *Political Theology*, 9.

[31]Dimitris Vardoulakis, "Stasis: Beyond Political Theology?," *Cultural Critique* 73 (Fall 2009): 125.

[32]See Emile Gentile, *Politics as Religion* (Princeton, NJ: Princeton University Press, 2006).

[33]For a careful and quantitative study of how this "value divide" has permeated American politics in the last quarter century, see Scott Keeter et al., *Trends in American Values: 1987–2012, Partisan Polarization Surges in Bush, Obama Years* (Washington, DC: Pew Research Center, 2012).

[34]See especially Talal Assad, *Genealogies of Religion: Discipline and Reasons of Power in Christianity and Islam* (Baltimore: Johns Hopkins University Press, 1993); Assad, *Formations of the Secular: Christianity, Islam, Modernity* (Stanford: Stanford University Press, 2003).

[35]The term *cultural Marxism* emerged during the 1980s as a term of derogation used by political conservatives in opposition to academic leftists. It has, however, been appropriated by some of the same leftist critics as a badge of honors. There is no reputable philosophical encylopedia or dictionary that offers a precise definition of the term, but generally it is used in popular and sometimes theoretical discourse to designate the extension of Marxist class analysis to culturally and historically marginalized populations that involve categories of gender, sexuality, religion and ethnicity. The notion of "women's liberation," for example, originally arose in the late 1960s out of this context. The various political movements—sometimes conflated under the general rubric of "identity politics"—over the past half century that have spawned what are commonly known as the "culture wars" can be attributed in many respects to the influence of cultural Marxism.

[36]The term *universalistic* is shorthand for what in philosophy is known as "moral universalism," a position first made precise by Kant. According to the Philosophy Index, "moral universalism" is "the position in meta-ethics that some moral values,

or moral system, can be applied universally to everyone—or at least everyone in similar circumstances. It is also known as universal morality, moderate moral realism or minimal moral realism, and is a form of ethical objectivism. Moral universalism holds that moral values apply to individuals regardless of their personal opinion, or the majority opinion of their culture. Other characteristics such as religion, race or gender are also excluded from moral judgements." http://www .philosophy-index.com/ethics/meta-ethics/universalism.php.

[37]Slavoj Žižek, "Multiculturalism, or the Cultural Logic of Multinational Capitalism," *New Left Review* 225 (1997): 46.

[38]"Slavoj Žižek on the Charlie Hebdo Massacre: Are the Worst Really Full of Passionate Intensity?," *New Statesman*, January 2015, 31, http://www.newstatesman.com/world -affairs/2015/01/slavoj-i-ek-charlie-hebdo-massacre-are-worst-really-full-passionate -intensity.

[39]Ibid.

[40]Immanuel Wallerstein, *European Universalism: The Rhetoric of Power* (New York: New Press), 71.

[41]Immanuel Wallerstein, "The Ideological Tensions of Capitalism: Universalism Versus Racism and Sexism," in Etienne Balibar and Immanuel Wallerstein, *Race, Nation, and Class: Ambiguous Identities* (New York: Verso, 1991), 30.

[42]Walter D. Mignolo, *Local Histories/Global Designs: Coloniality, Subaltern Knowledges, and Border Thinking* (Princeton, NJ: Princeton University Press, 2000), 87.

[43]Ibid., 297.

[44]Walter D. Mignolo, *The Darker Side of Western Modernity: Global Futures. Decolonial Options* (Durham, NC: Duke University Press, 2011), 144.

[45]Ibid., 83.

CHAPTER 4: THE QUESTION OF RELIGION

[1]Max Horkheimer and Theodor W. Adorno, *Dialectic of Enlightenment: Philosophical Fragments*, ed. Gunzelin Schmid Noerr, trans. Edmund Jephcott, Cultural Memory in the Present (Stanford: Stanford University Press, 2002), 69.

[2]Ibid., 70.

[3]Immanuel Kant, *Groundwork of the Metaphysics of Morals*, ed. and trans. Mary Gregor and Jens Timmerman (Cambridge: Cambridge University Press, 2011), 71.

[4]Horkheimer and Adorno, *Dialectic of Enlightenment*, 71.

[5]John Locke, *An Essay Concerning Human Understanding* 2.21.31.

[6]Horkheimer and Adorno, *Dialectic of Enlightenment*, 115.

[7]The concept of "situationism" can be traced to the writing and cultural practices of the French avant-garde theorist Duy Debord, who founded the "Situationist International." Debord insisted that the term was meaningless as an ideological construct

and thus resisted all precise definition. However, in one of his writings he referred to it as "a mode of experimental behavior" linked to the conditions of urban society: "a technique of rapid passage through varied ambiances." Guy Debord, "Theory of the Dérive," in *Visual Culture: Critical Concepts in Media and Cultural Studies,* ed. Joanne Morra and Marquard Smith, vol. 3 (New York: Routledge, 2006), 77. Debord focused on the use of certain "artistic interventions" that disrupted the familiarity, predictability and monotony of urban life. It is the parent concept for such familiar, contemporary urban practices as street mime and flash mobs.

[8]According to *The Urban Dictionary,* culture jamming "is the act of using existing media such as billboards, bus-ads, posters, and other ads to comment on those very media themselves or on society in general, using the original medium's communication method. It is based on the idea that advertising is little more than propaganda for established interests, and that there is little escape from this propaganda in industrialized nations. Culture jamming differs from artistic appropriation (which is done for art's sake), and from vandalism where destruction or defacement is the primary goal." http://www.urbandictionary.com/define.php?term=culture%20jam.

[9]See Guy Debord, *The Society of the Spectacle* (Eastbourne, UK: Soul Bay Press, 2009).

[10]Karl Marx, *Critique of Hegel's Philosophy of Right,* ed. Joseph O'Malley (Cambridge: Cambridge University Press, 1977), 131.

[11]Slavoj Žižek, *The Puppet and the Dwarf: The Perverse Core of Christianity* (Cambridge, MA: MIT Press, 2003), 6.

[12]Slavoj Žižek, *The Fragile Absolute: Or, Why Is the Christian Legacy Worth Fighting For?* (New York: Verso, 2000).

[13]Slavoj Žižek, *On Belief* (New York: Routledge, 2001).

[14]Slavoj Žižek and John Milbank, *The Monstrosity of Christ: Paradox or Dialectic?,* ed. Creston Davis (Cambridge, MA: MIT Press, 2009).

[15]Slavoj Žižek, *Absolute Recoil: Towards A New Foundation Of Dialectical Materialism* (London: Verso, 2014), 29.

[16]Alain Badiou, *St. Paul: The Foundation of Universalism,* trans. Ray Brassier (Stanford: Stanford University Press, 2003), 1-2.

[17]Ibid., 2.

[18]Ibid., 4.

[19]Ibid.

[20]Ibid., 6.

[21]Ibid., 14-15.

[22]Ibid., 45.

[23]Ibid.

[24]Ibid., 70.

[25]Ibid., 53.

[26]Ibid., 55.

[27]Ibid., 56.

[28]Ibid., 75.

[29]Ibid., 76-77.

[30]Ibid., 81.

[31]Ibid., 149.

[32]Ibid., 154.

[33]Ibid.

[34]Ibid., 160.

[35]Ibid.

[36]Ibid., 80.

[37]Ibid., 88.

[38]Ibid., 89.

[39]Ibid., 90.

[40]Ibid. 98.

[41]Žižek, *The Puppet and the Dwarf*, 13.

[42]Ibid., 87.

[43]Ibid., 118.

[44]Slavoj Žižek, "Dialectical Conceit Versus the Misty Conceit of Paradox," in Slavoj Žižek and John Milbank, *The Monstrosity of Christ: Paradox or Dialectic?*, ed. Creston Davis (Cambridge, MA: MIT Press, 2009), 254.

[45]Interview with Slavoj Žižek, *The Believer*, July 2004, http://www.believermag.com/issues/200407/?read=interview_zizek.

[46]Ibid.

[47]Ibid.

[48]Žižek, "Dialectical Conceit," 303.

CHAPTER 5: TOWARD A THEOLOGY OF THE "RELIGIOUS"

[1]Margarete Kohlenbach and Raymond Geuss, "Introduction: The Frankfurt School and the Problem of Religion," in *The Early Frankfurt School and Religion*, ed. Margarete Kohlenbach and Raymond Geuss (New York: Palgrave Macmillan, 2005), 1. Other scholars argue that the Frankfurt school as a whole took religion much more seriously than many conventionally assume. See, for example, Eduardo Mendieta, *The Frankfurt School on Religion: Key Writings by the Major Thinkers* (London: Routledge, 2005). Up through the 1930s the Frankfurt school itself adhered largely to the orthodox Marxist view of religion as the "sigh of the oppressed." After atheism became the official ideology of Soviet Communism, however, the Frankfurt school slowly adopted the view that religious commitment might also be a form of

resistance to state power. A good summary of this more nuanced approach can be found in Christopher Craig Brittain, "The Frankfurt School on Religion," *Religion Compass* 6 (March 2012): 204-12.

[2]Carl Raschke, "Religious Studies and the Default of Critical Intelligence," *Journal of the American Academy of Religion* 54 (1986): 131-38.

[3]See Martin Marty, "A Life of Learning," *Occasional Papers of the American Council of Learned Societies* 62 (2006): 13.

[4]See Robert Ellwood, *Alternative Altars: Unconventional and Eastern Spirituality in America* (Chicago: University of Chicago Press, 1979).

[5]See Hent de Vries, *Philosophy and the Turn to Religion* (Baltimore: Johns Hopkins University Press, 1999).

[6]Perry Anderson, *The Origins of Postmodernity* (New York: Verso, 1998), 62.

[7]Baudrillard's most important work is *Simulacra and Simulation*, trans. Sheila Faria Glaser (Ann Arbor: University of Michigan Press, 1994). See also Baudrillard, *Cool Memories*, vol. 4, *1995–2000*, trans. Chris Turner (London: Verso, 2003).

[8]The term *postdenominational* was coined by Fuller Seminary professor Peter C. Wagner in the mid-1990s. See his *The New Apostolic Churches* (Ventura, CA: Regal, 1998).

[9]See John Ankerberg and John Weldon, *The Encyclopedia of New Age Beliefs* (Eugene, OR: Harvest House, 1996), 116

[10]See Lydia Bean, *The Politics of Evangelical Identity: Local Churches and Partisan Divides in the United States and Canada* (Princeton, NJ: Princeton University Press, 2014), 53.

[11]Richard Murphy, *Theorizing the Avant-Garde* (Cambridge: Cambridge University Press, 1999), 272.

[12]Jack Goody, *Representations and Contradictions: Ambivalence Towards Images, Theatre, Fictions, Relics, and Sexuality* (Oxford: Blackwell, 1997).

[13]This insight was actually discovered by Émile Durkheim. In the *Elementary Forms of Religious Life*, Durkheim notes that the synecdochal relationship between part and whole is the basis of the sense of "sacrality." "A mere fragment of the flag represents the Motherland just as well as the flag itself. Therefore, it is sacred in the same way and to the same degree." *Durkheim on Religion*, ed. W. S. F. Pickering, AAR Texts and Translations 6 (Atlanta: Scholars Press, 1994), 139.

[14]Gary Genosko, *Undisciplined Theory* (Thousand Oaks, CA: Sage, 1998), 151.

[15]See Stephen Gersh, *Concord in Discourse: Harmonics and Semiotics in Late Classical and Early Medieval Platonism* (Berlin: de Gruyter, 1996).

[16]The literature on critical theory of religion is not extensive, but it is significant. Like the word *postmodern*, the terms *critical* or *critical theoretical* are often used in widely diverging and sometimes idiosyncratic ways. The most important recent contribu-

tions can be found in the work of Rudolf Siebert. See Rudolf Siebert, *The Critical Theory of Religion: The Frankfurt School* (Lanham, MD: Scarecrow, 2001); Siebert, *Manifesto of the Critical Theory of Society and Religion: The Wholly Other, Liberation, Happiness, and the Rescue of the Hopeless* (Leiden: Brill, 2010); Marc P. Lalonde, *From Critical Theology to a Critical Theory of Religious Insight: Essays in Contemporary Religious Thought* (Bern: Peter Lang, 2007); Graham Ward, *Theology and Contemporary Critical Theory* (New York: Macmillan, 2000); Marsha Hewitt, *Critical Theory of Religion: A Feminist Analysis* (Minneapolis: Fortress, 1995); Warren S. Goldstein, *Marx, Critical Theory, and Religion: A Critique of Rational Choice* (Leiden: Brill, 2009).

[17]See Karl Barth's famous statement in *Church Dogmatics* that "religion is unbelief. It is a concern, indeed, we must say that it is the one great concern, of godless man." Barth, *Church Dogmatics*, ed. Geoffrey W. Bromiley and T. F. Torrance, trans. Geoffrey W. Bromiley (Edinburgh: T&T Clark, 1956), I/2:299.

[18]See Tomoko Masuzawa, *The Invention of World Religions, Or How European Universalism Was Preserved in the Language of Pluralism* (Chicago: University of Chicago Press, 2012).

[19]The closest thing to a definition of biopolitics by Foucault can be found in his "Course Semmary" in his lectures during the academic year 1978–1979. Biopolitics is, Foucault writes, "the attempt, starting with the eighteenth century, to rationalize the problems posed to government practice by phenomena consisting of a set of living beings forming a population: health, hygiene, birthrate, life expectancy, race." *The Birth of Biopolitics: Lectures at the Collège de France, 1978–1979* (New York: Picador Reprints, 2010), 317.

[20]See Carl Raschke, *Force of God: Political Theology and the Crisis of Liberal Democracy* (New York: Columbia University Press, 2015).

[21]This argument was first made in a trenchant and powerful manner by Jacques Derrida in his essay from the late 1960s titled "Force and Signification," which many would consider the founding document of "deconstruction" as well as "post-structuralism." See Jacques Derrida, "Force and Signification," in *Writing and Difference*, trans. Alan Bass (Chicago: University of Chicago Press, 1978), 5-30. Also see Raschke, *Force of God*, chap. 2, "Force of Thought."

CHAPTER 6: WHAT FAITH REALLY MEANS IN A TIME OF GLOBAL CRISIS

[1]Craig Calhoun, Mark Juergensmeyer and Jonathan VanAntwerpen, introduction to *Rethinking Secularism*, ed. Craig Calhoun, Mark Juergensmeyer and Jonathan VanAntwerpen (New York: Oxford University Press, 2011), 8.

[2]Ibid.

[3]José Casanova, "The Secular, Secularizations, Secularisms," in Calhoun, Juergensmeyer and VanAntwerpen, *Rethinking Secularism*, 68.

[4]Ibid., 55.

[5]One needs to consider the reflections of Charles Taylor here. "'What do we mean when we speak of Western modernity as secular'? There are all sorts of ways of describing it: the separation of religion from the public life, the decline of religious belief and practice. But while one cannot avoid touching on these, my main interest here lies in another facet of our age: belief in God, or in the transcendent in any form, is contested; it is an option among many; it is therefore fragile; for some people in some milieus, it is very difficult, even 'weird.' Five hundred years ago in Western civilization, this wasn't so. Unbelief was off the map, close to inconceivable, for most people." Taylor, "Western Secularity," in Calhoun, Juergensmeyer and VanAntwerpen, *Rethinking Secularism*, 50. Taylor's major work on secularism (often considered his magnum opus) is *A Secular Age* (Cambridge, MA: Belknap Press of Harvard University Press, 2007). Earlier works include Taylor, *Modern Social Imaginaries* (Durham, NC: Duke University Press, 2004); and Taylor, *The Sources of the Self: The Making of Modern Identity* (Cambridge, MA: Cambridge University Press, 1989).

[6]Casanova, "The Secular, Secularizations, Secularisms," 55.

[7]See Ulrich Beck, *A God of One's Own: Religion's Capacity for Peace and Potential for Violence*, trans. Rodney Livingstone (New York: Polity, 2010). Other works by Beck include *Cosmopolitan Vision* (Hoboken, NJ: Wiley, 2014); and Beck, *Power in the Global Age: A New Global Political Economy* (Hoboken, NJ: Wiley, 2014).

[8]Andrew Greeley, "After Secularity: The Neo-Gemeinschaft Society: A Post-Christian Postscript," *Sociology of Religion* 27 (1966): 126.

[9]Massimo Rossati and Kristina Stoeckl, introduction to *Global Connections: Multiple Modernities and Post-secular Societies*, ed. Massimo Rossati and Kristina Stoeckl (Farnham, UK: Ashgate, 2012), 3.

[10]Vincent Geoghegan, "Religious Narrative, Post-secularism and Utopia," *Critical Review of International and Social Political Philosophy* 3 (2000): 205-24.

[11]Philip S. Gorski, David Kyuman Kim, John Torpey and Jonathan VanAntwerpen, *The Post-Secular in Question* (New York: New York University Press, 2012), 2.

[12]Geoghegan, "Religious Narrative, Post-secularism and Utopia," 206.

[13]Kristina Stoeckl, *"Defining the Postsecular"* (paper presented at the Academy of Sciences in Moscow, February 2011), http://synergia-isa.ru/wp-content/uploads/2012/02/stoeckl_en.pdf.

[14]Richard John Neuhaus, "Educational Diversity in Post-secular America," *Religious Education* 77, no. 3 (1982): 309.

[15]Stoeckl, "Defining the Postsecular."

[16]Jürgen Habermas, "Notes on a Post-secular Society," 19, http://www.staff.amu.edu.pl/~ewa/Habermas,%20Notes%20on%20Post-Secular%20Society.pdf.

[17]Ibid.

[18]Jürgen Habermas, "On the Relation Between the Secular Liberal State and Religion," in *Political Theologies: Public Religions in a Post-secular World,* ed. Hent de Vries and Lawrence E. Sullivan (New York: Fordham University Press, 2006), 258.

[19]See particularly Olivier Roy, *Holy Ignorance: When Religion and Culture Part Ways* (New York: Oxford University Press, 2014).

[20]My translation.

[21]Ulrich Beck, *Power in the Global Age: A New Global Political Economy* (Hoboken, NJ: Wiley, 2014), Kindle edition, loc. 7840-41.

[22]Ibid., loc. 7877.

[23]Ibid., loc. 7903.

[24]Ibid., loc. 7911.

[25]See again my *Force of God.*

[26]Roy, *Holy Ignorance,* xiii.

[27]Jean Baudrillard and Sylvère Lotringer, *The Ecstasy of Communication* (New York: Autonomedia, 1988), 101.

Author Index

Subject Index

Finding the Textbook You Need

The IVP Academic Textbook Selector
is an online tool for instantly finding the IVP books
suitable for over 250 courses across 24 disciplines.

---

www.ivpress.com/academic/
